ISBN 978-1-4584-2348-1

7777 W. BLUEMOUND RD. P.O. BOX 13819 MILWAUKEE, WI 53213

For all works contained herein:
Unauthorized copying, arranging, adapting, recording, Internet posting, public performance,
or other distribution of the printed music in this publication is an infringement of copyright.
Infringers are liable under the law.

Visit Hal Leonard Online at
www.halleonard.com

CONTENTS

4 Blackbird
THE BEATLES

9 City of New Orleans
ARLO GUTHRIE, WILLIE NELSON

14 Don't Let the Rain Come Down
THE SERENDIPITY SINGERS

18 The 59th Street Bridge Song (Feelin' Groovy)
SIMON & GARFUNKEL, HARPERS BIZARRE

24 Green Green Grass of Home
TOM JONES, PORTER WAGONER

21 Greenback Dollar
THE KINGSTON TRIO

26 Greenfields
THE BROTHERS FOUR

30 Guantanamera
THE SANDPIPERS

32 The House of the Rising Sun
THE ANIMALS

34 Lemon Tree
TRINI LOPEZ

37 Midnight Special
CREEDENCE CLEARWATER REVIVAL

40 The M.T.A.
THE KINGSTON TRIO

43 Puff the Magic Dragon
PETER, PAUL & MARY

46 Rock Island Line
HUDDIE LEDBETTER, LONNIE DONEGAN

48 San Francisco Bay Blues
JESSE FULLER, ERIC CLAPTON

61 Scotch and Soda
THE KINGSTON TRIO

50 Sloop John B.
THE KINGSTON TRIO

52 Son-of-a-Preacher Man
DUSTY SPRINGFIELD

56 Tom Dooley
THE KINGSTON TRIO

58 26 Miles (Santa Catalina)
THE FOUR PREPS

64 The Unicorn
THE IRISH ROVERS

70 Walk Right In
THE ROOFTOP SINGERS

67 We'll Sing in the Sunshine
GALE GARNETT

76 Where Have All the Flowers Gone?
PETE SEEGER, THE KINGSTON TRIO

72 Wishin' and Hopin'
DUSTY SPRINGFIELD

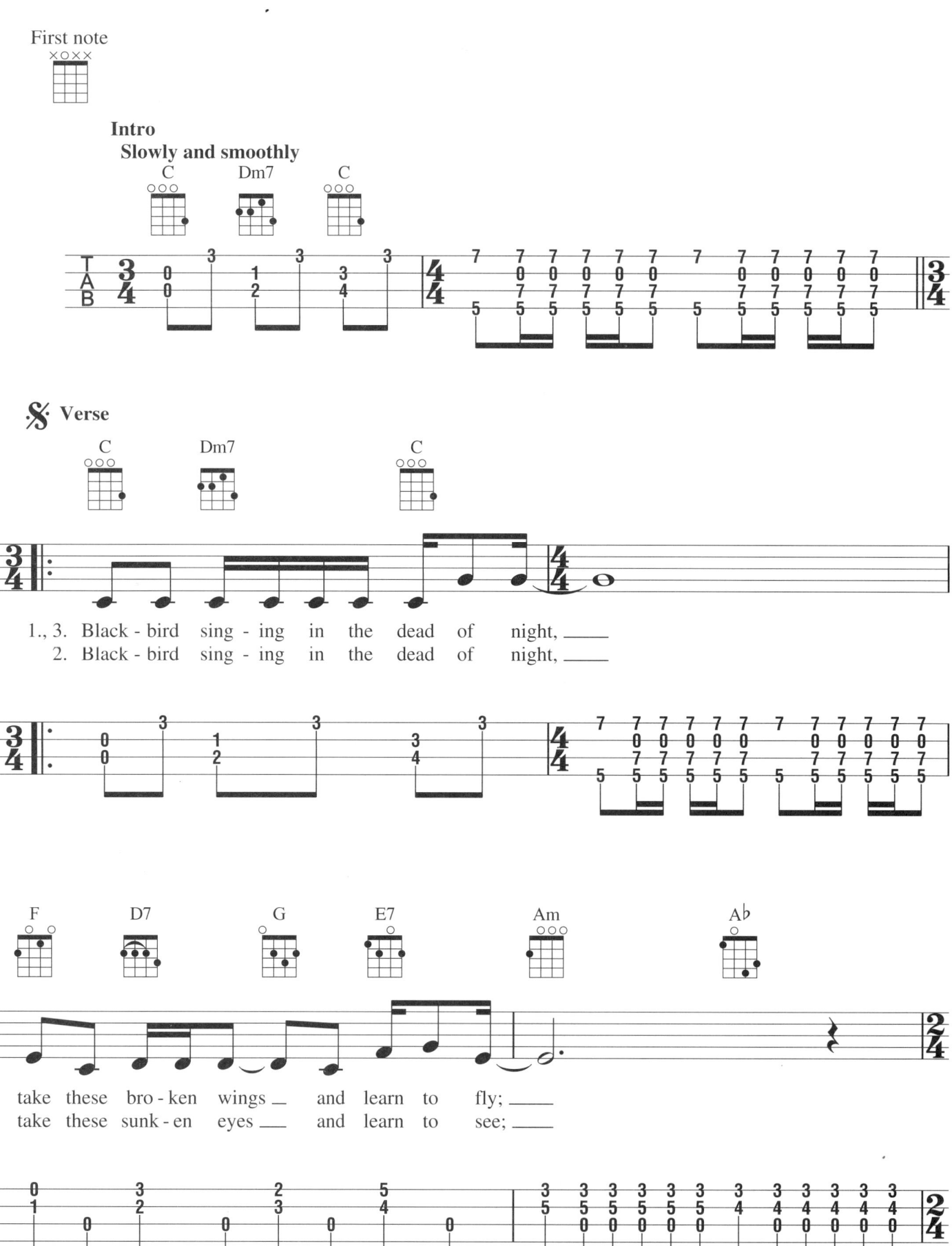

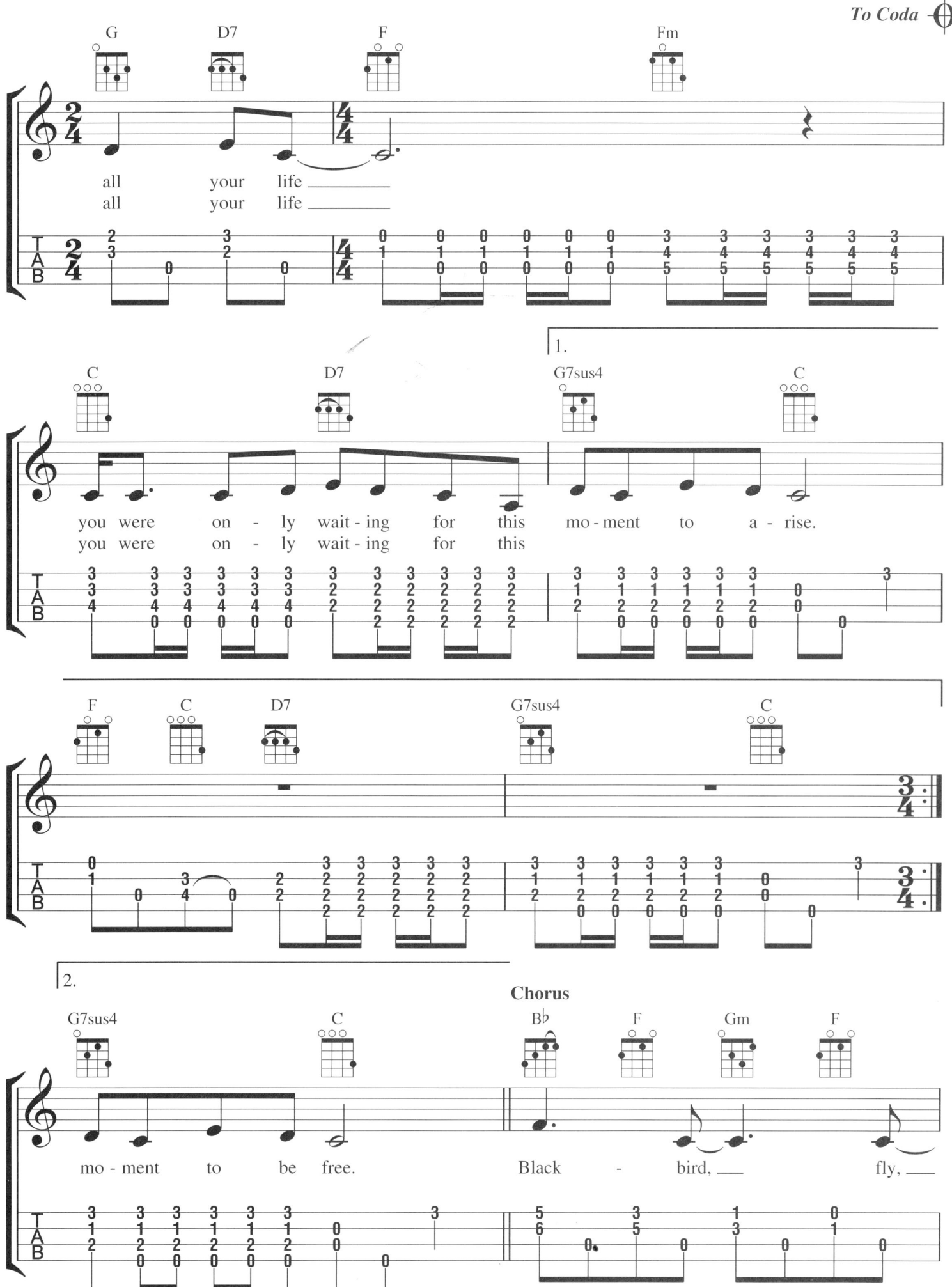

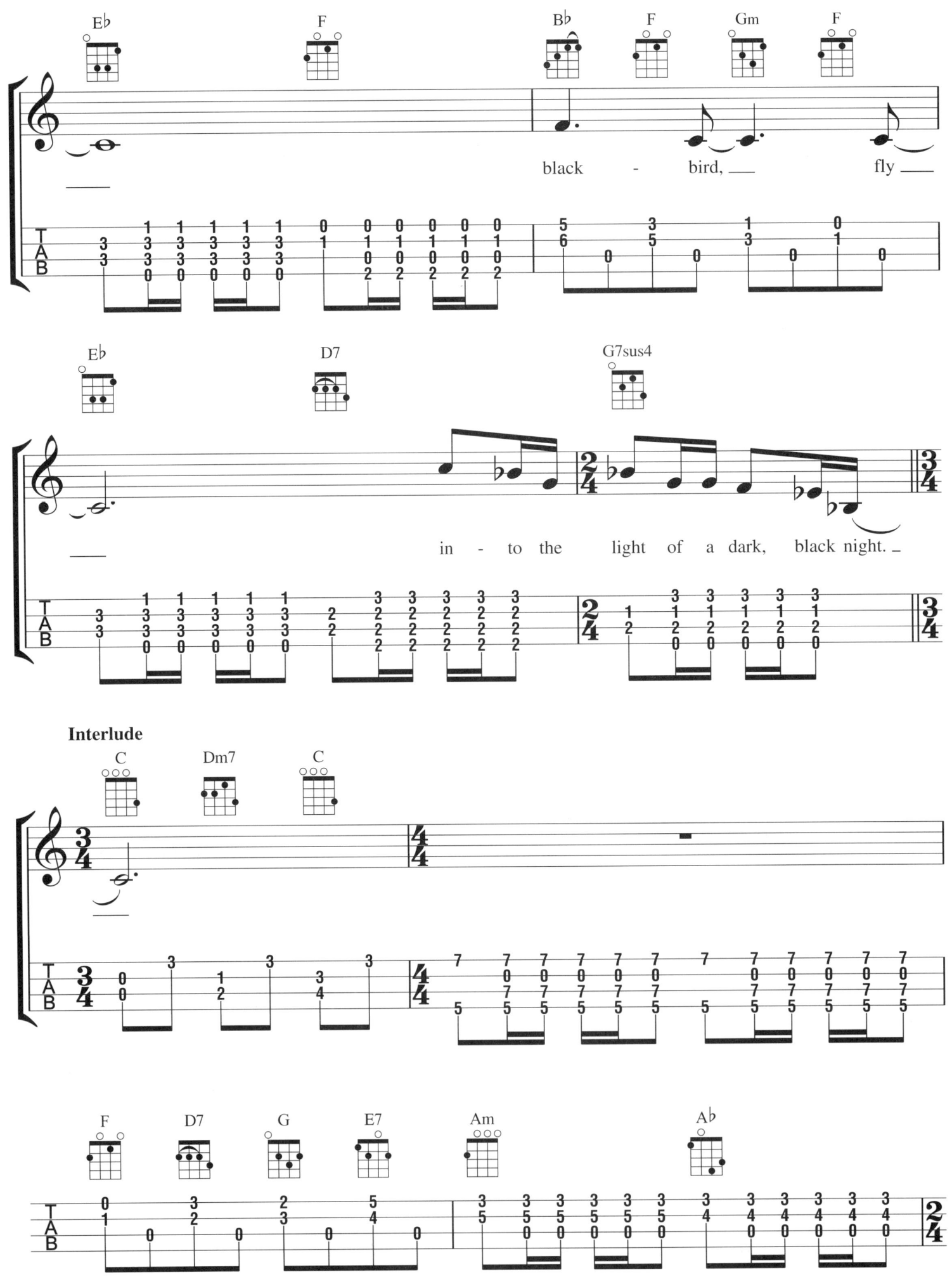

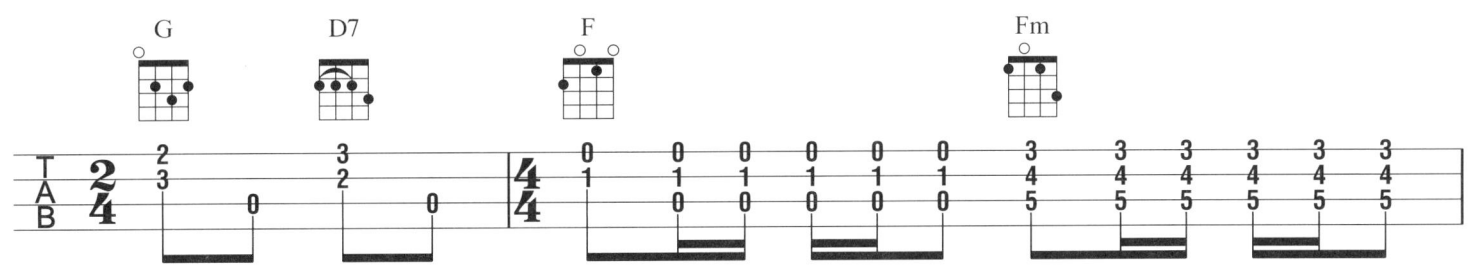
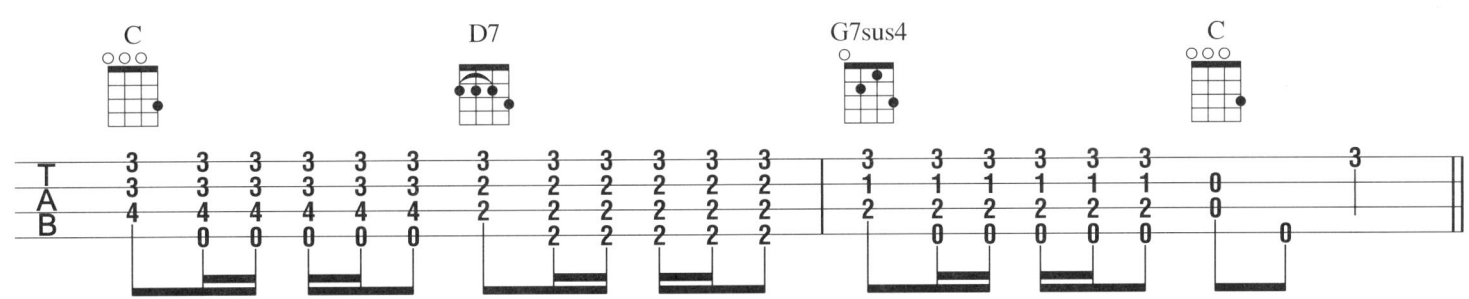

Chorus

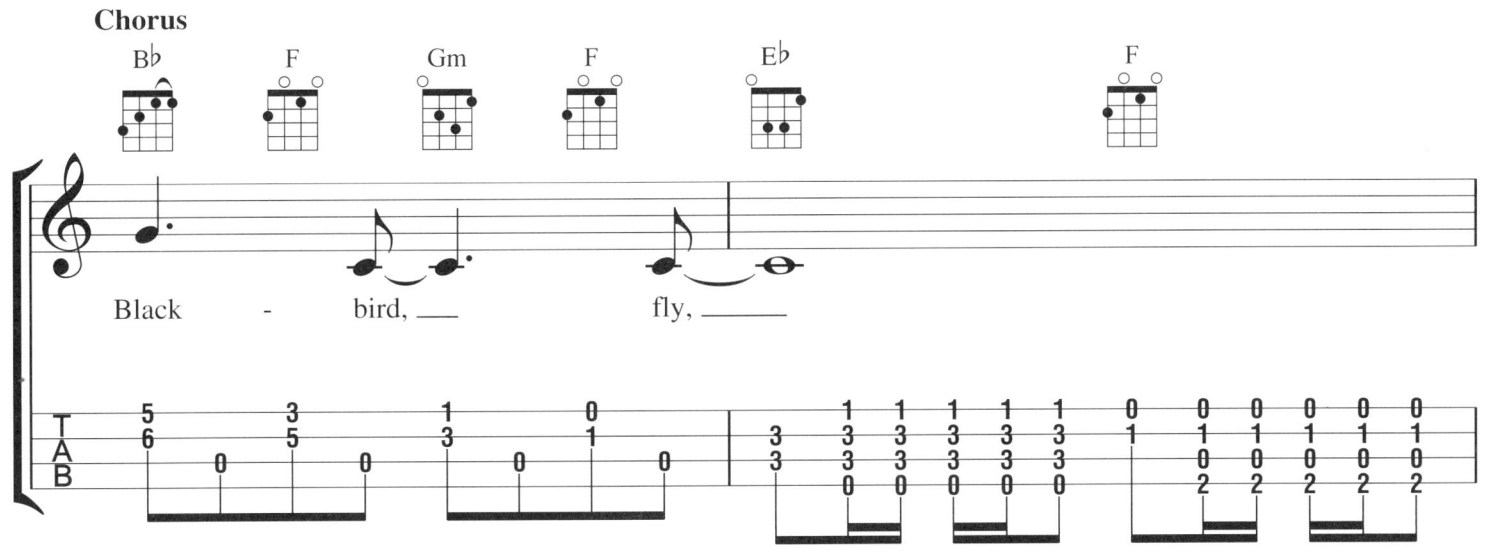

Black - bird, ___ fly, ___

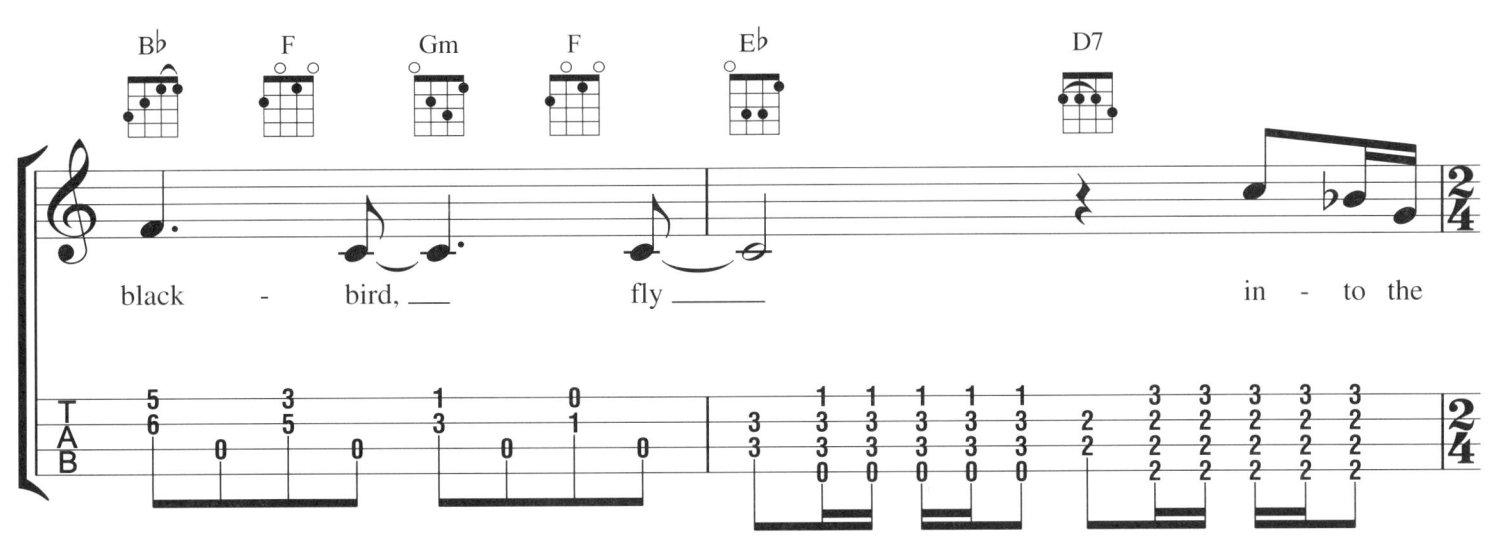

black - bird, ___ fly ___ in - to the

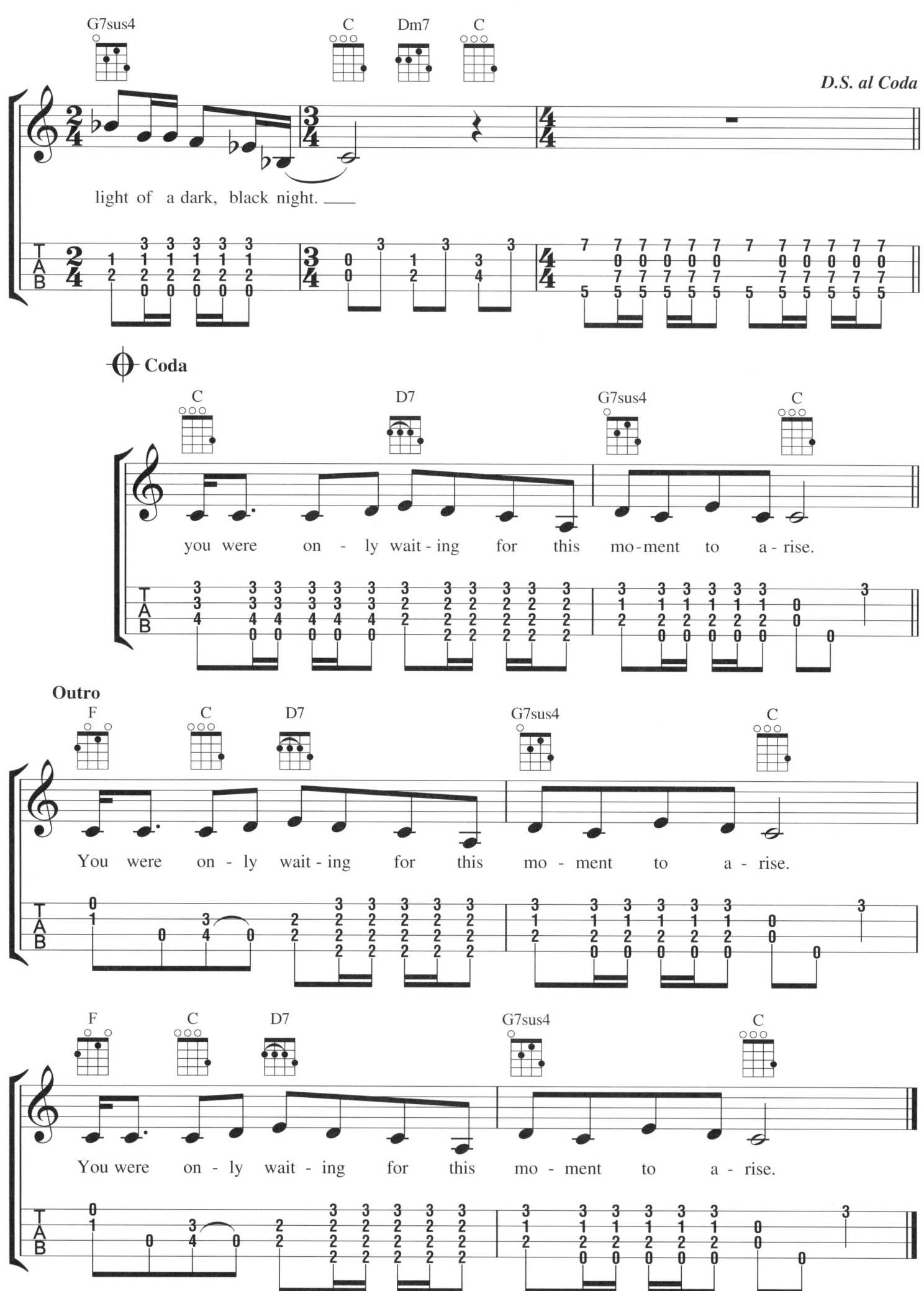

City of New Orleans

Words and Music by Steve Goodman

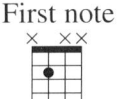
First note

Verse
Moderately bright Country tempo

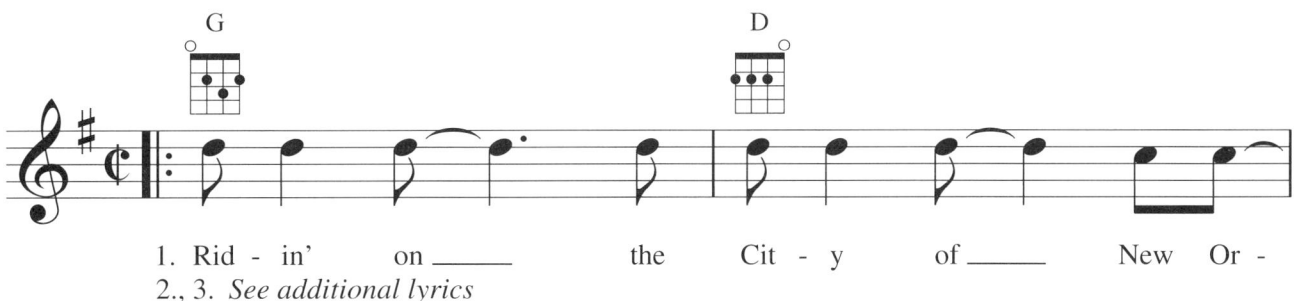

1. Rid - in' on ____ the Cit - y of ____ New Or -
2., 3. *See additional lyrics*

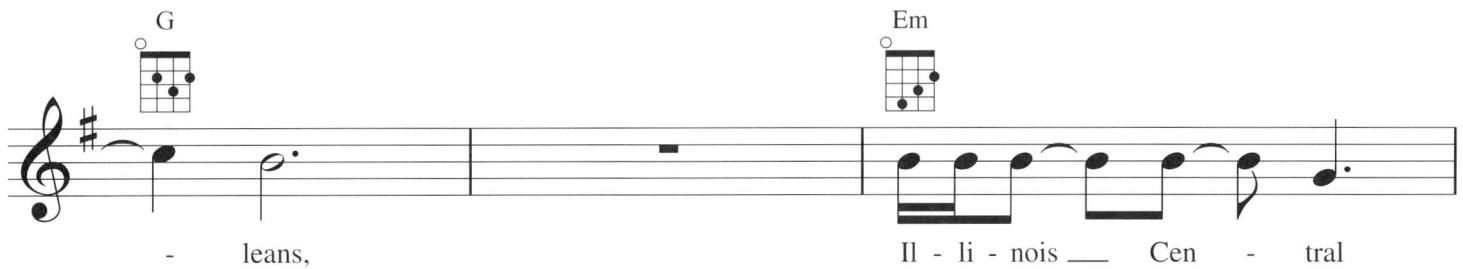

- leans, Il - li - nois ____ Cen - tral

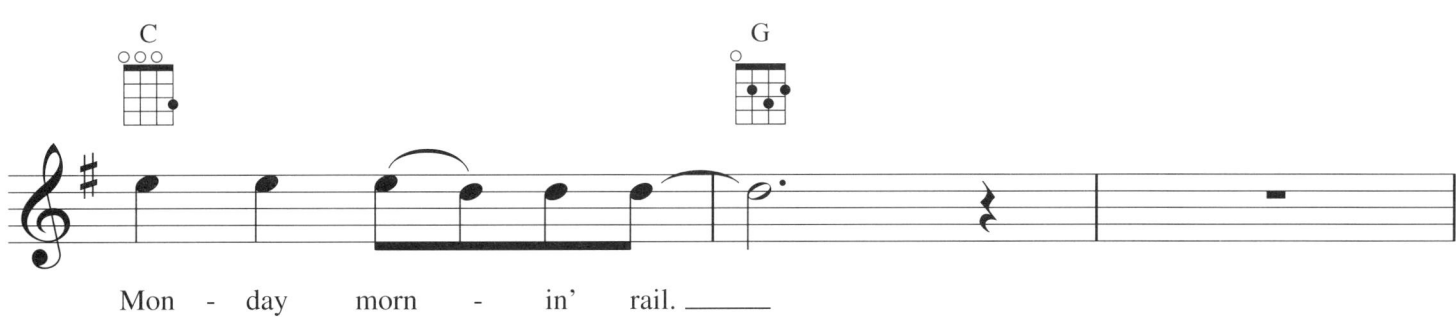

Mon - day morn - in' rail. ____

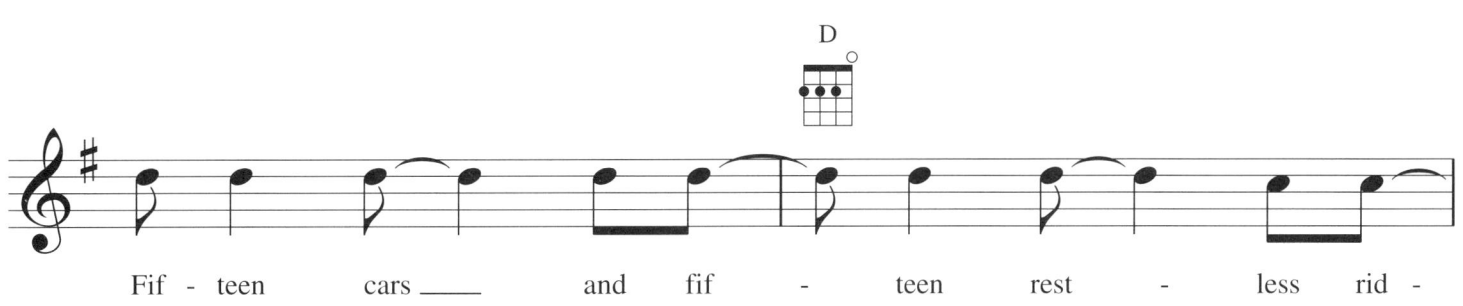

Fif - teen cars ____ and fif - teen rest - less rid -

Copyright © 1970 (Renewed 1998), 1971 (Renewed 1999) JURISDAD MUSIC and TURNPIKE TOM MUSIC
All Rights Reserved   International Copyright Secured   Used by Permission
www.stevegoodman.net

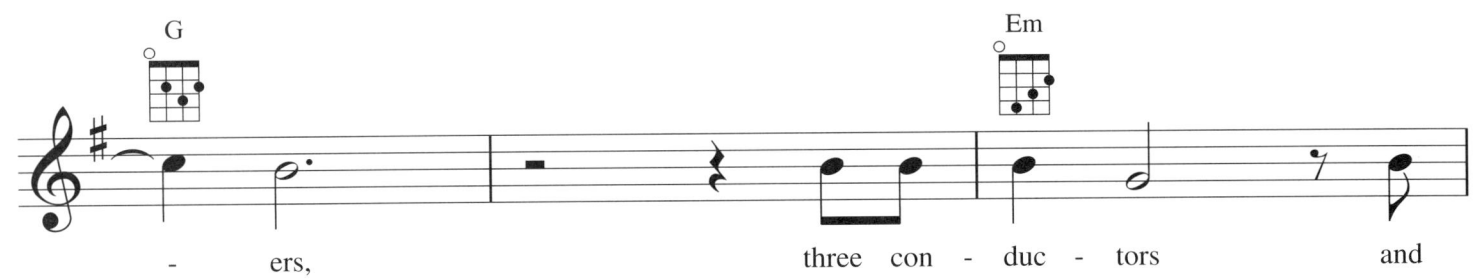
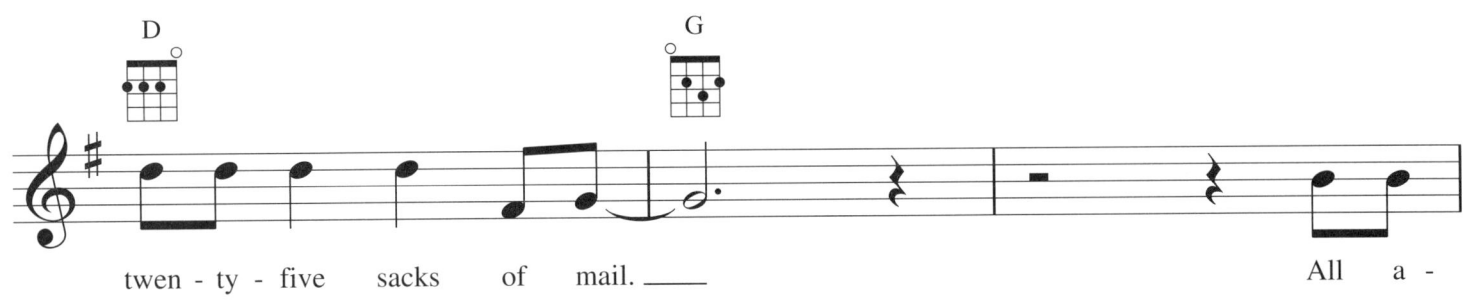
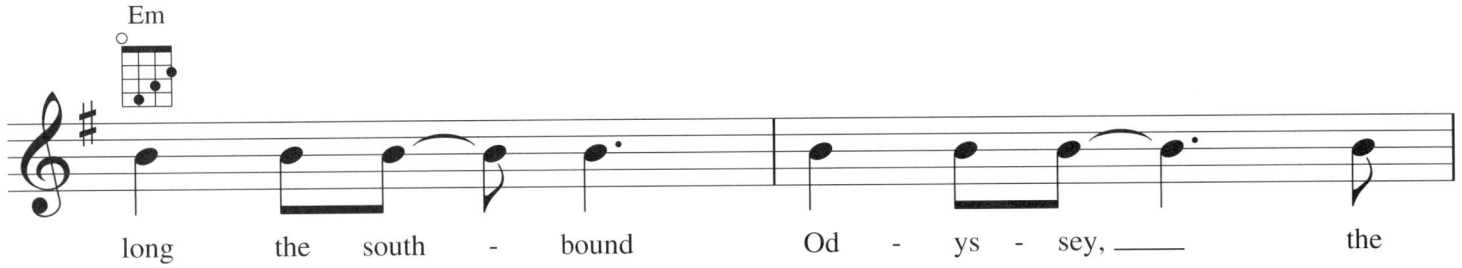
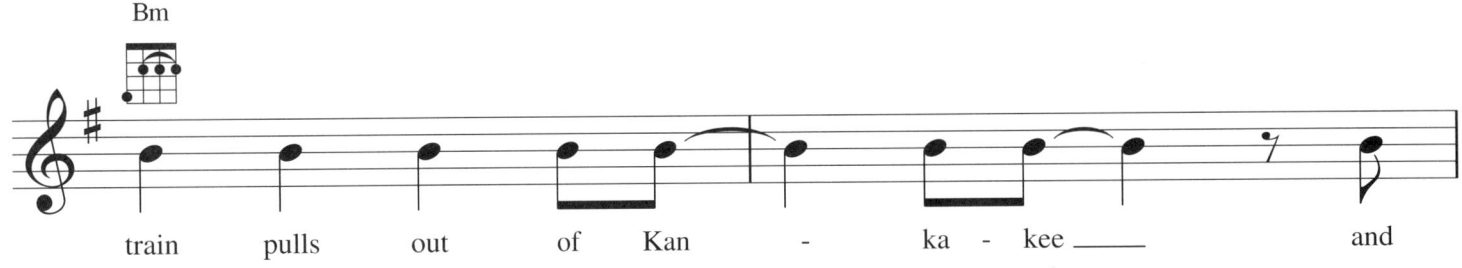
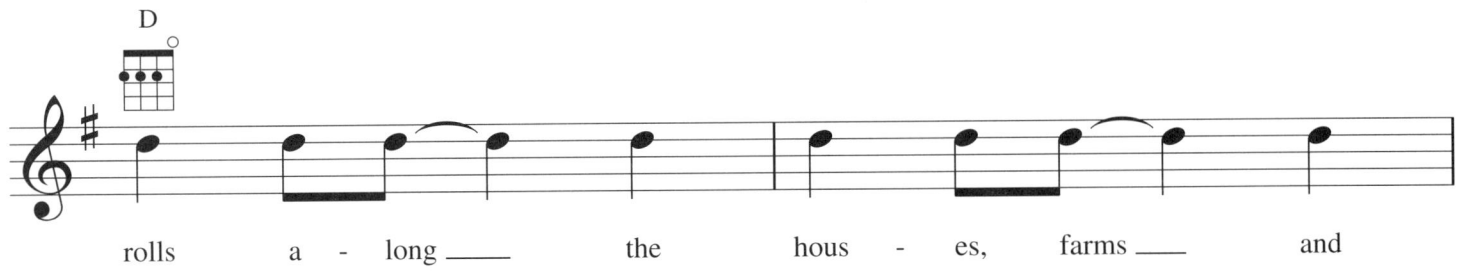

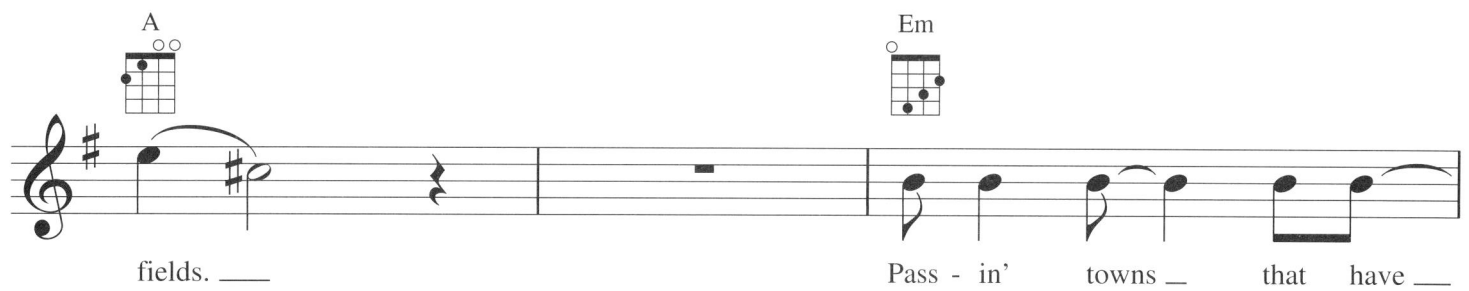
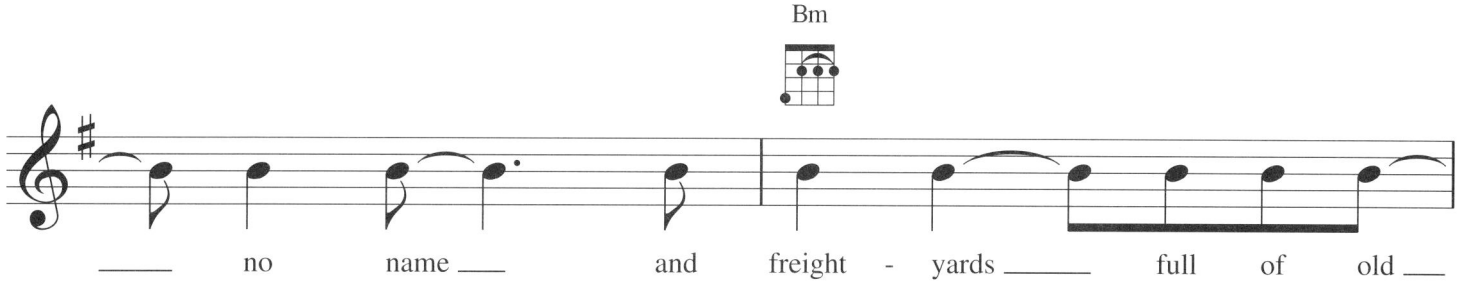
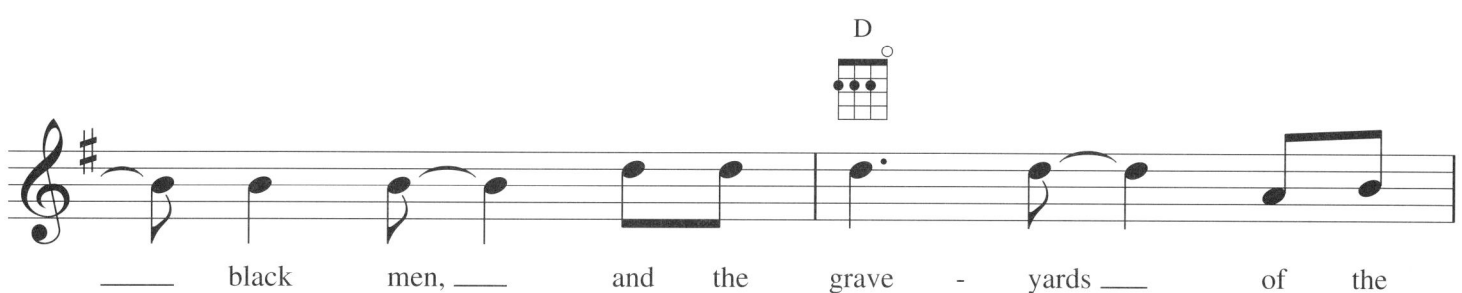
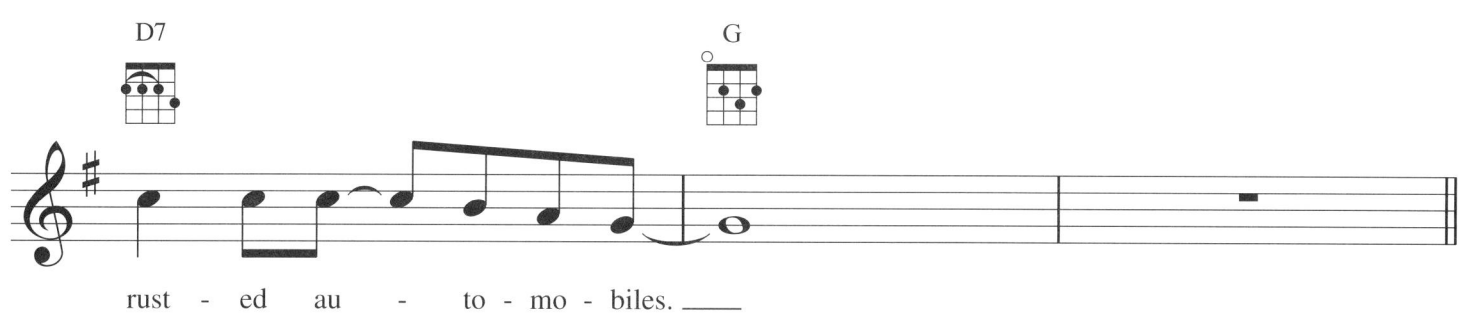
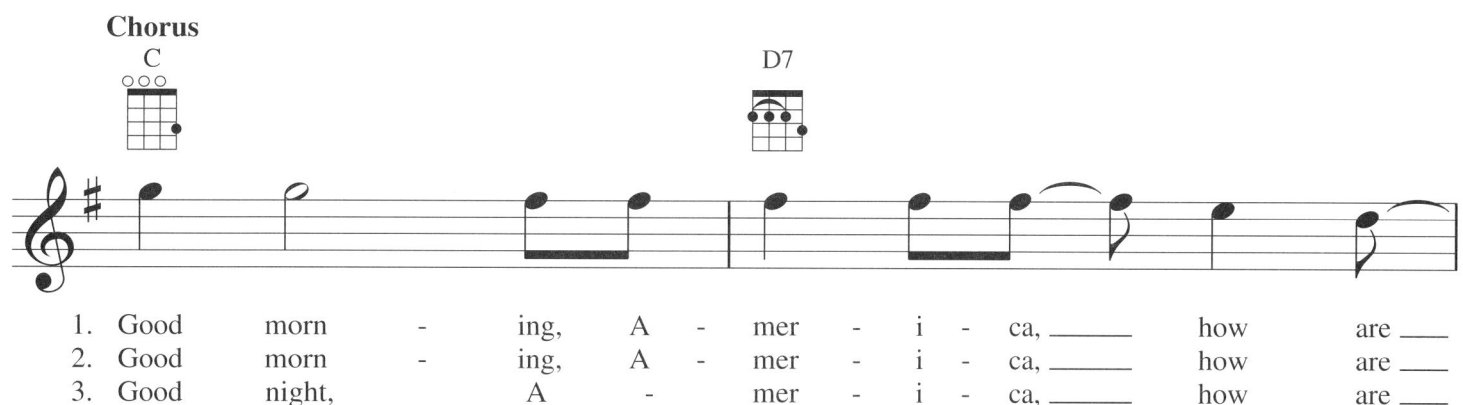

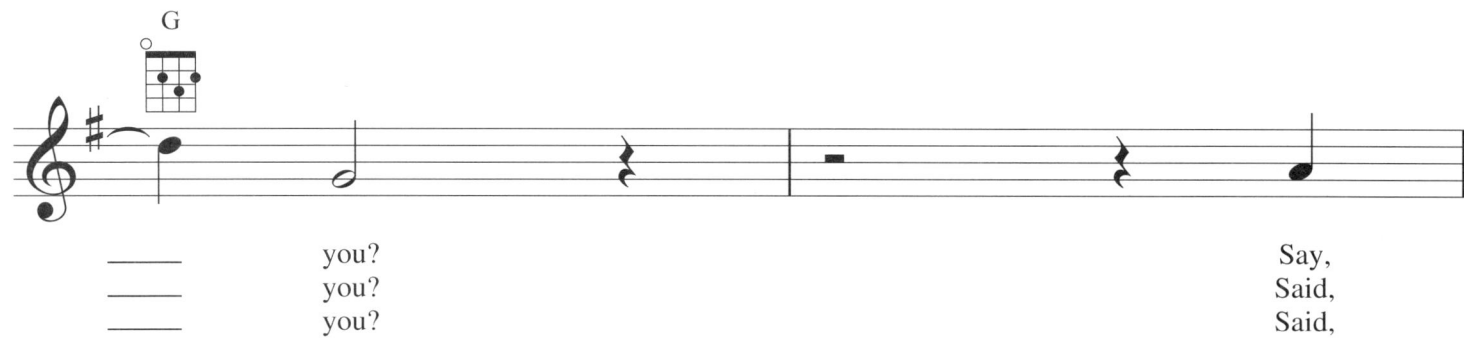
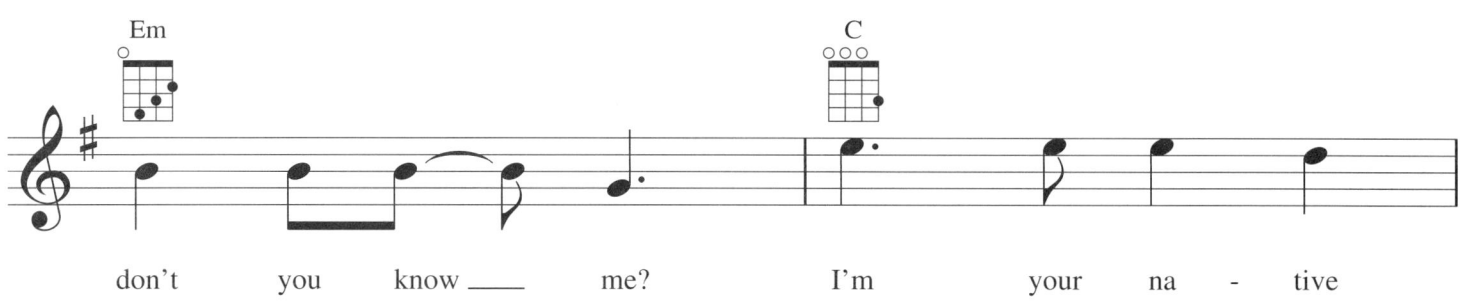
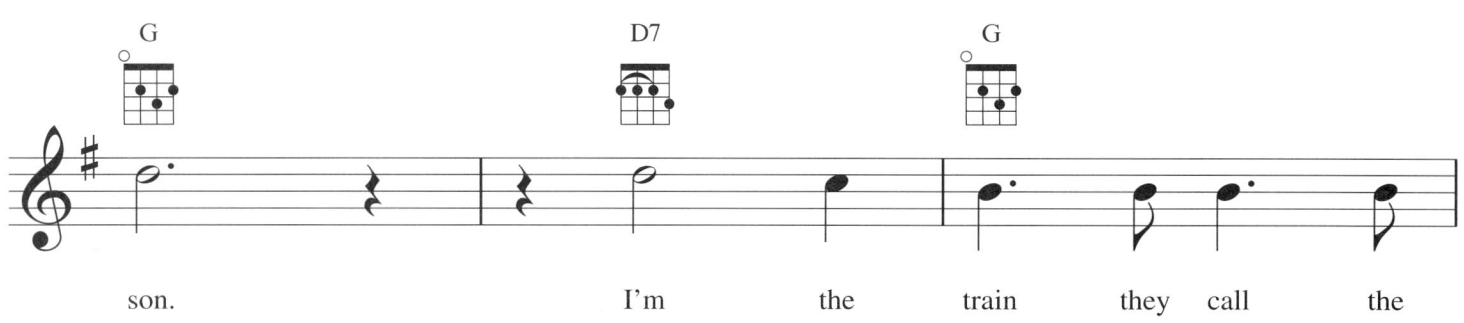
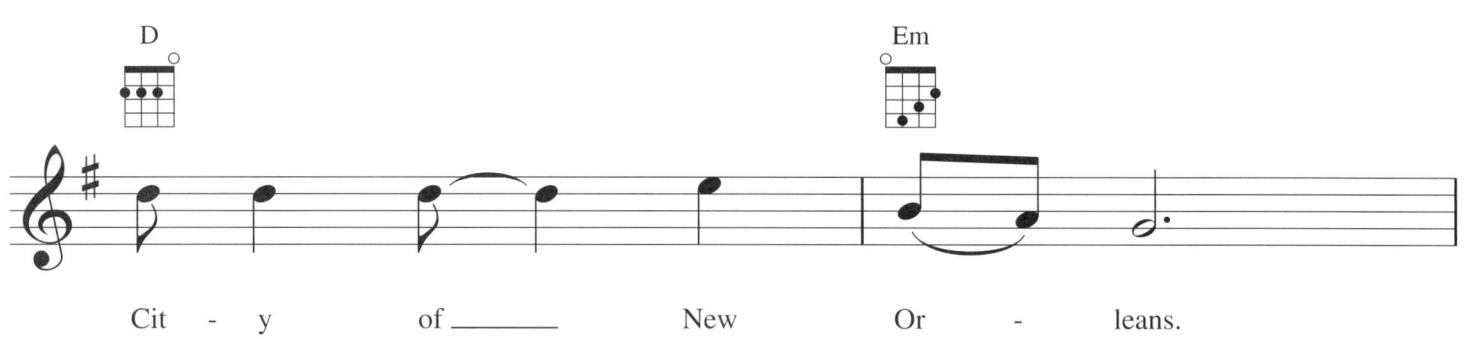
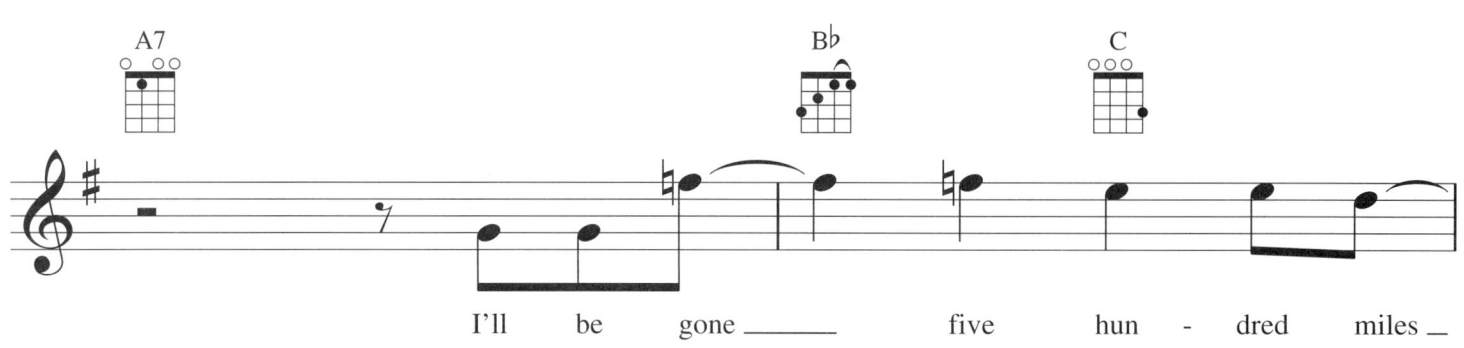

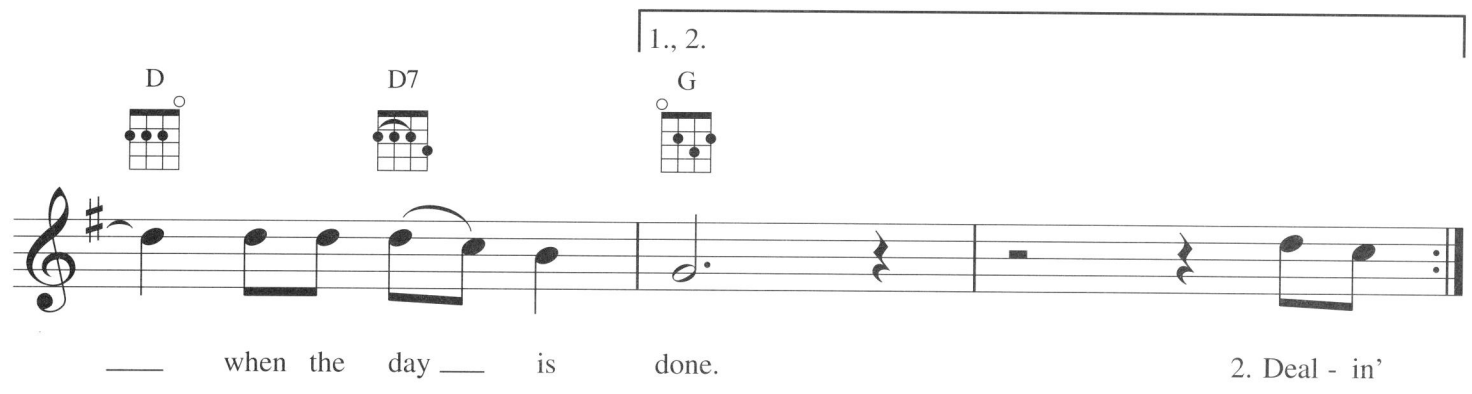

Additional Lyrics

2. Dealin' card games with the old men in the club car,
   Penny a point, ain't no one keepin' score.
   Pass the paper bag that holds the bottle;
   Feel the wheels grumblin' 'neath the floor.
   And the sons of Pullman porters, and the sons of engineers
   Ride their father's magic carpet made of steel.
   Mothers with their babes asleep are rockin' to the gentle beat,
   And the rhythm of the rails is all they feel.

3. Night time on the City of New Orleans,
   Changin' cars in Memphis, Tennessee.
   Halfway home, we'll be there by mornin',
   Thru the Mississippi darkness rollin' down to the sea.
   But all the towns and people seem to fade into a bad dream,
   And the steel rail still ain't heard the news.
   The conductor sings his songs again;
   The passengers will please refrain,
   This train's got the disappearin' railroad blues.

Don't Let the Rain Come Down
(Crooked Little Man) (Crooked Little House)

Words and Music by Ersel Hicky and Ed E. Miller

First note
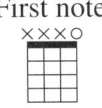

Moderate Calypso

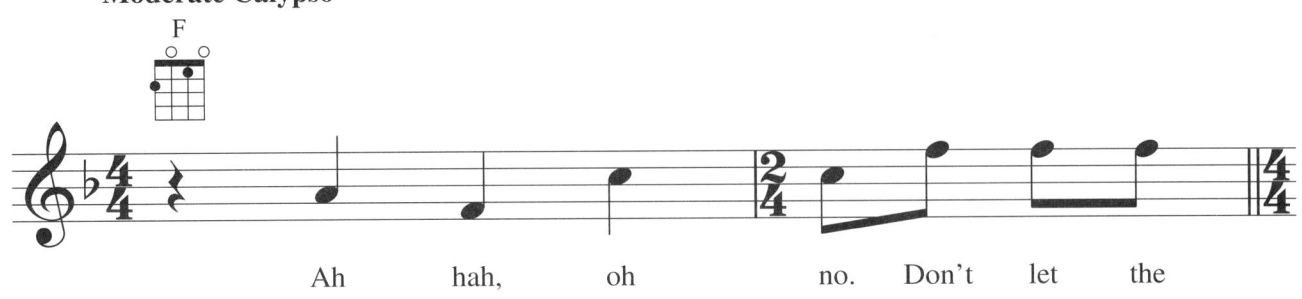

Ah hah, oh no. Don't let the

𝄋 **Chorus**

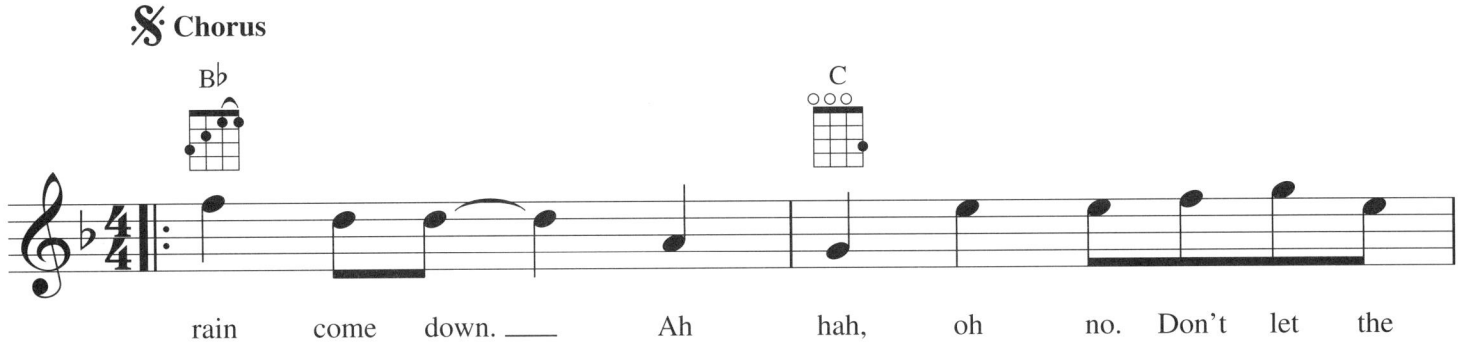

rain come down. Ah hah, oh no. Don't let the

rain come down. Ah hah, oh no. Don't let the

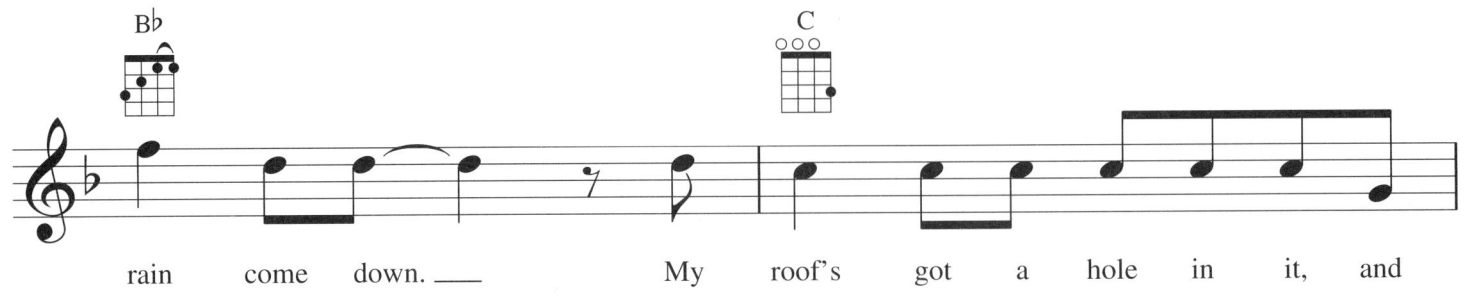

rain come down. My roof's got a hole in it, and

© 1960 (Renewed 1988) SCREEN GEMS-EMI MUSIC INC. and SERENDIPITY PUBLISHING CORP.
All Rights Controlled and Administered by SCREEN GEMS-EMI MUSIC INC.
All Rights Reserved   International Copyright Secured   Used by Permission

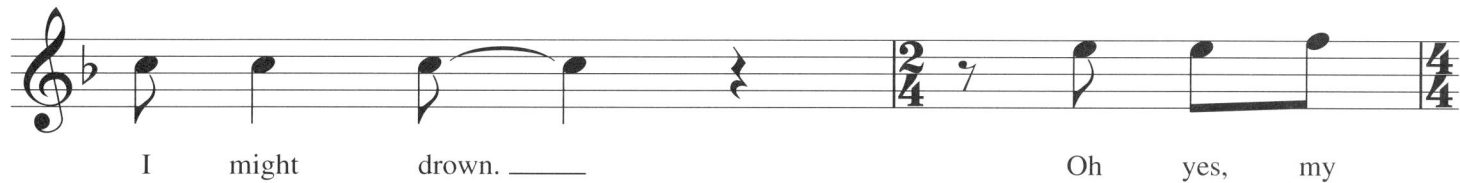

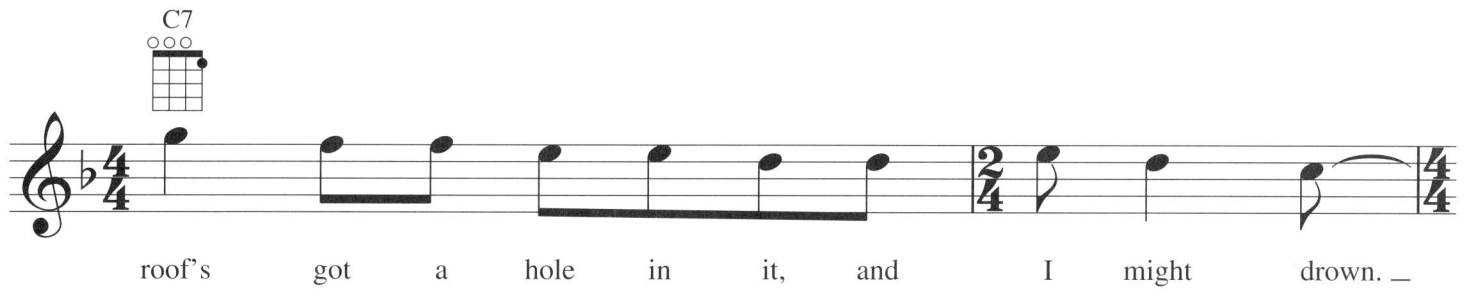
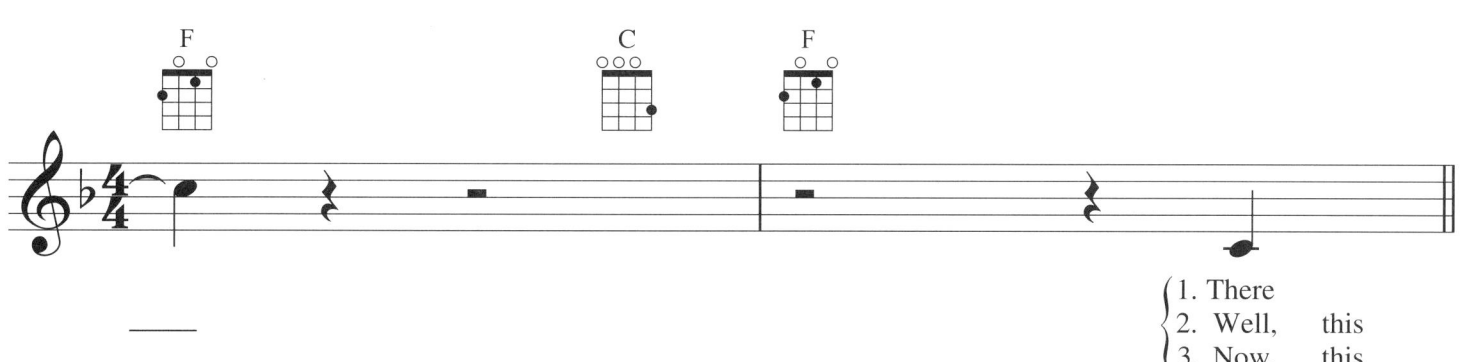

Verse

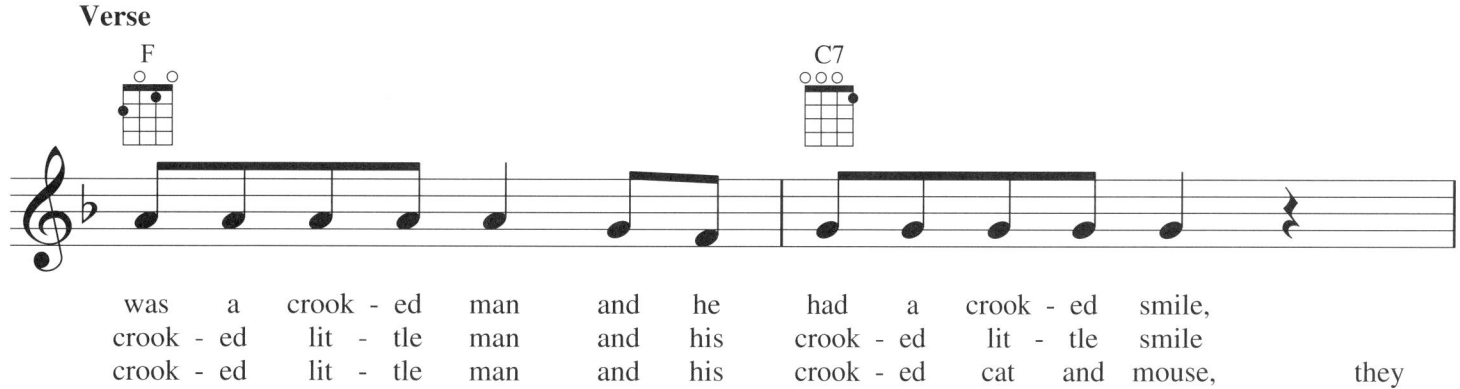
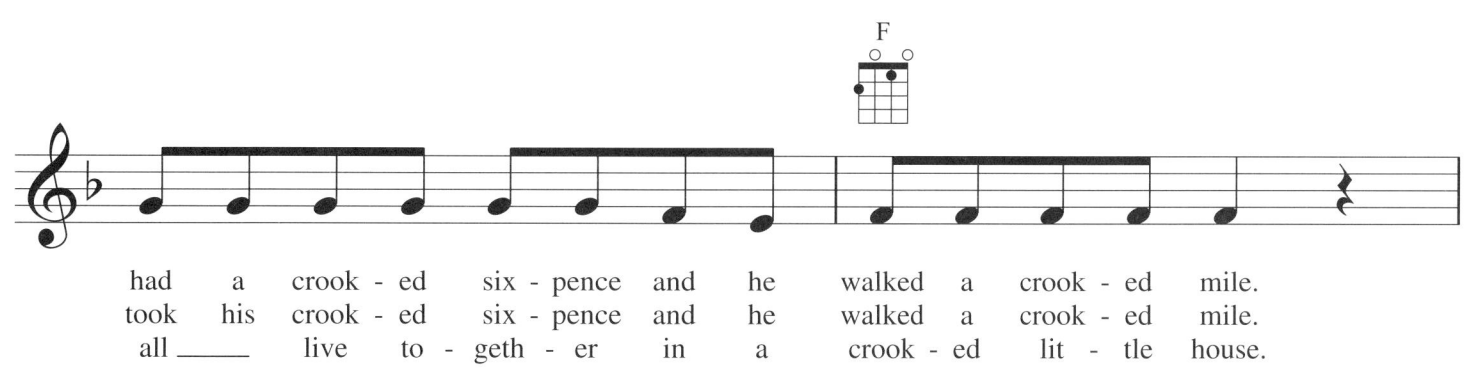

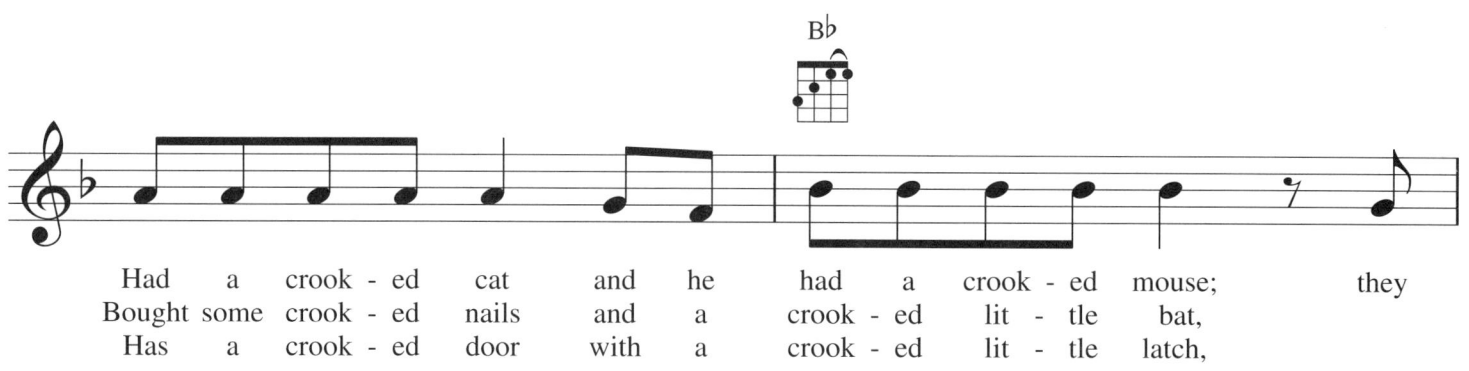
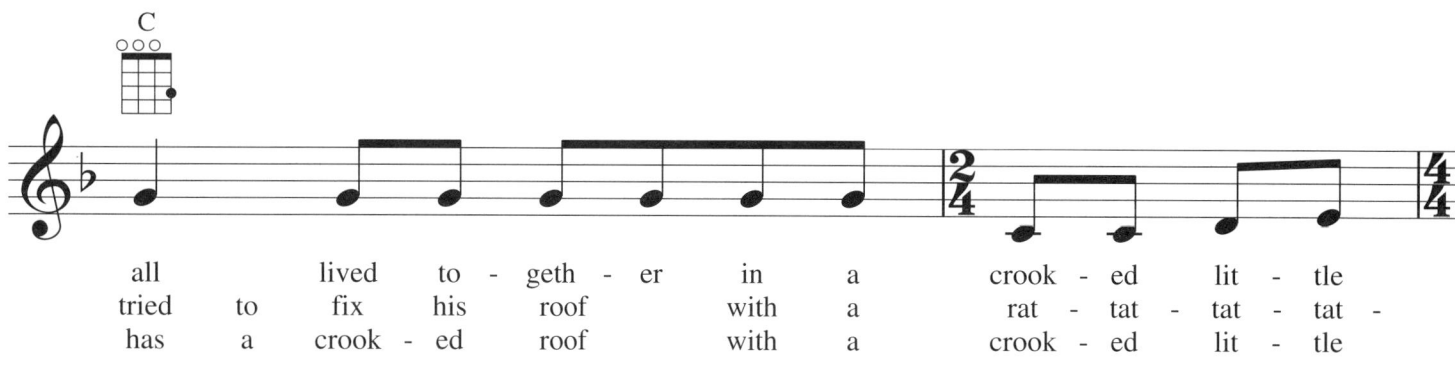
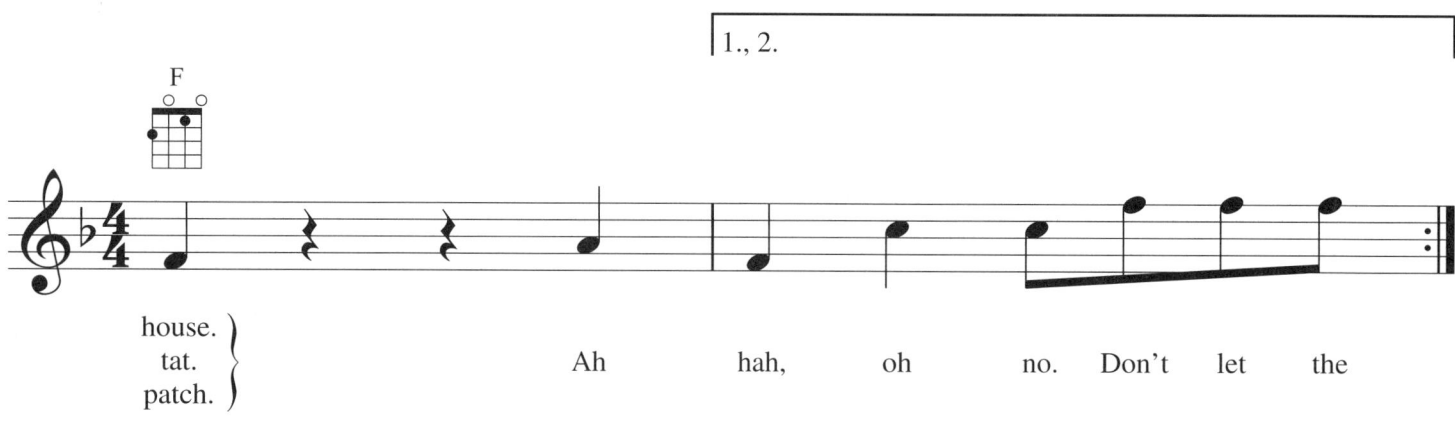
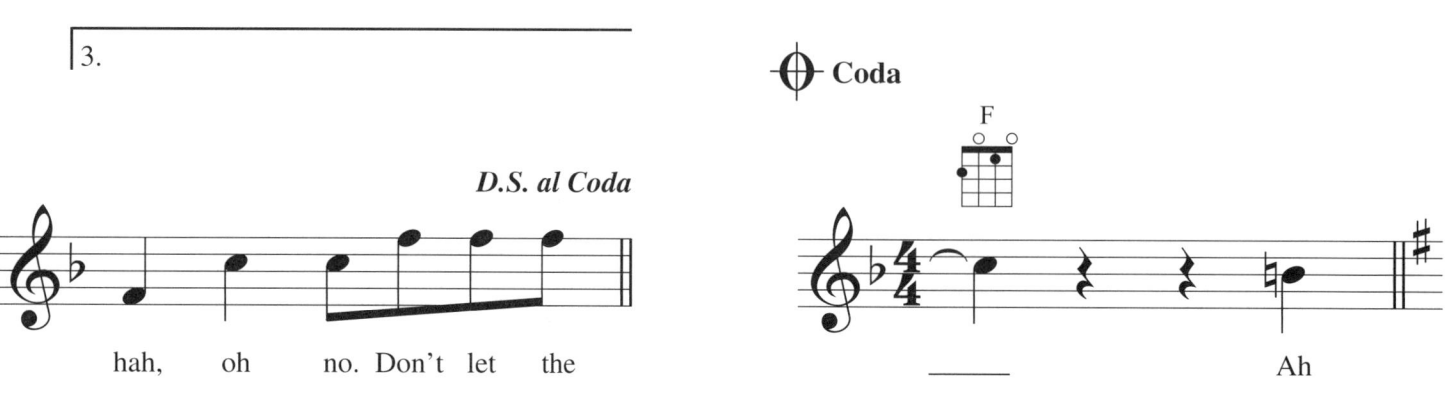

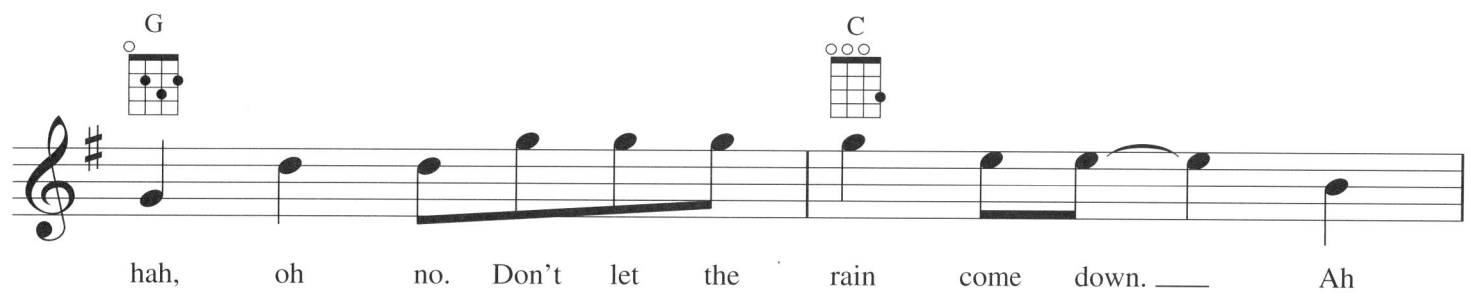
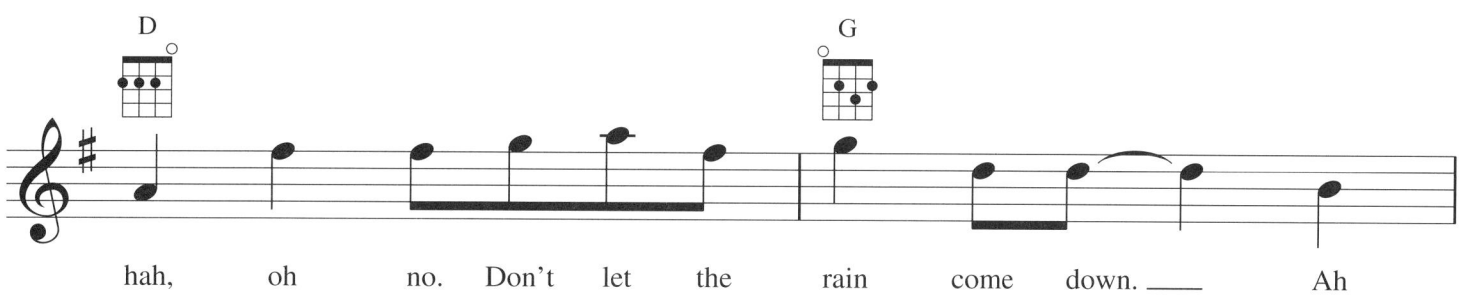
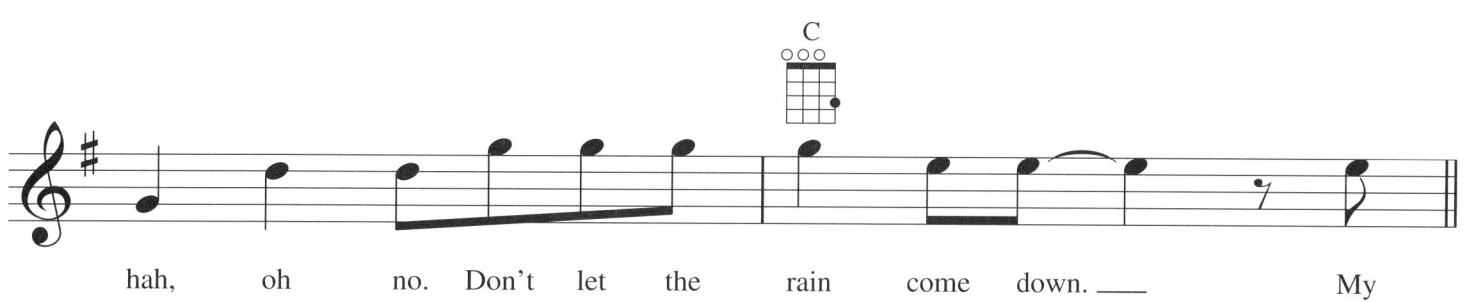

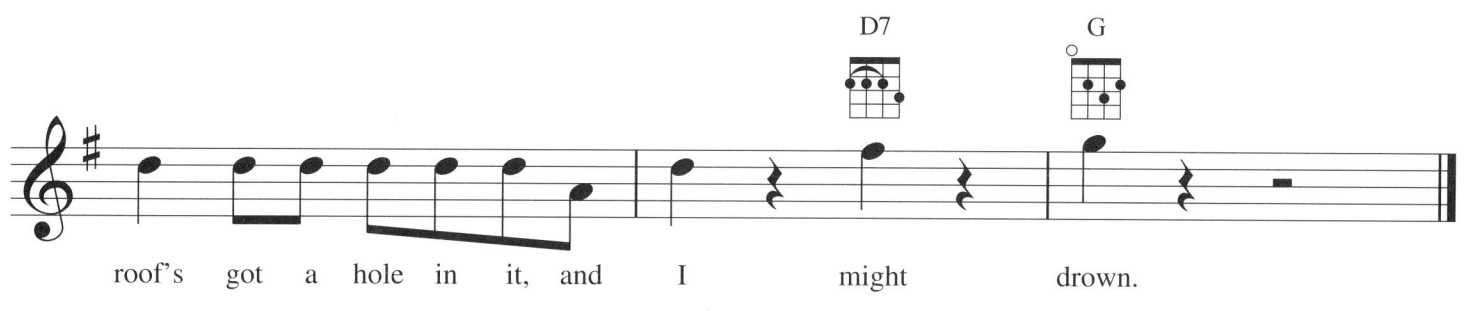

The 59th Street Bridge Song
(Feelin' Groovy)
Words and Music by Paul Simon

First note

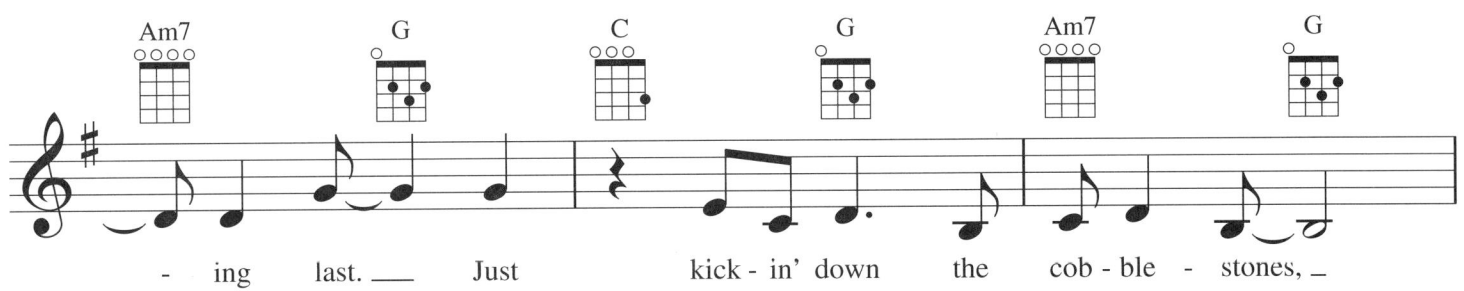

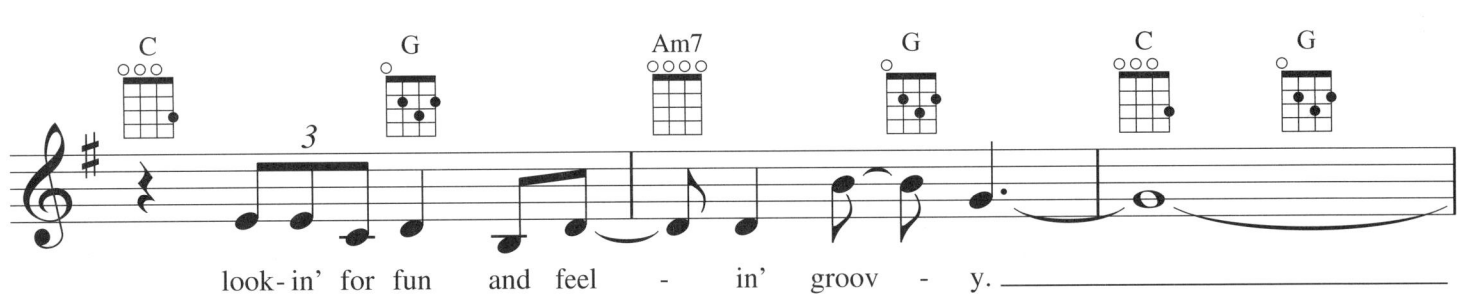

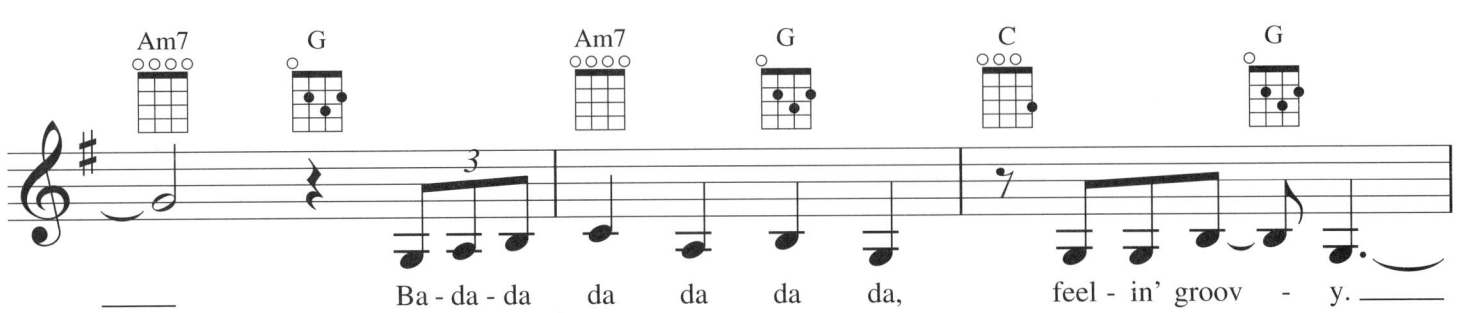

Copyright © 1966, 1967 Paul Simon (BMI)
International Copyright Secured   All Rights Reserved
Used by Permission

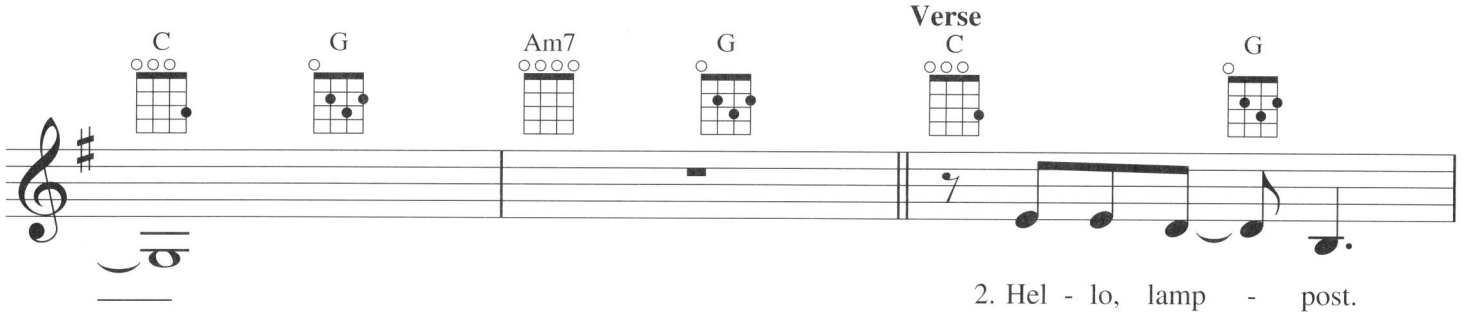

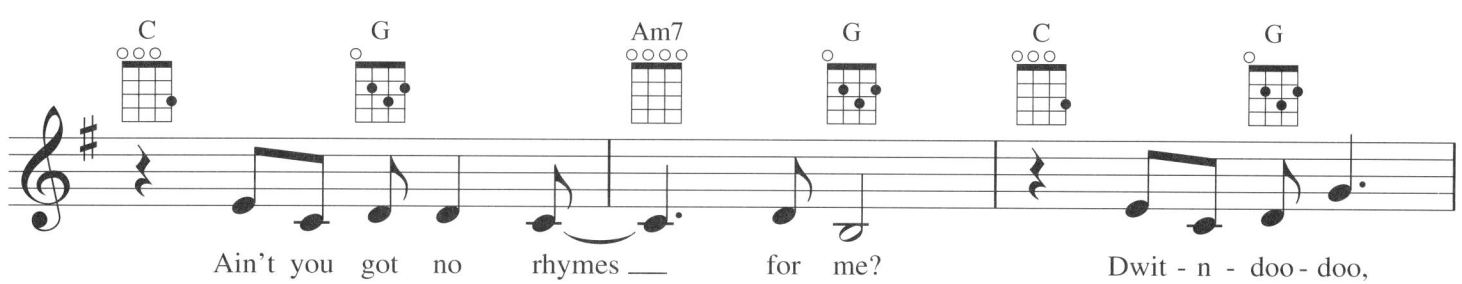
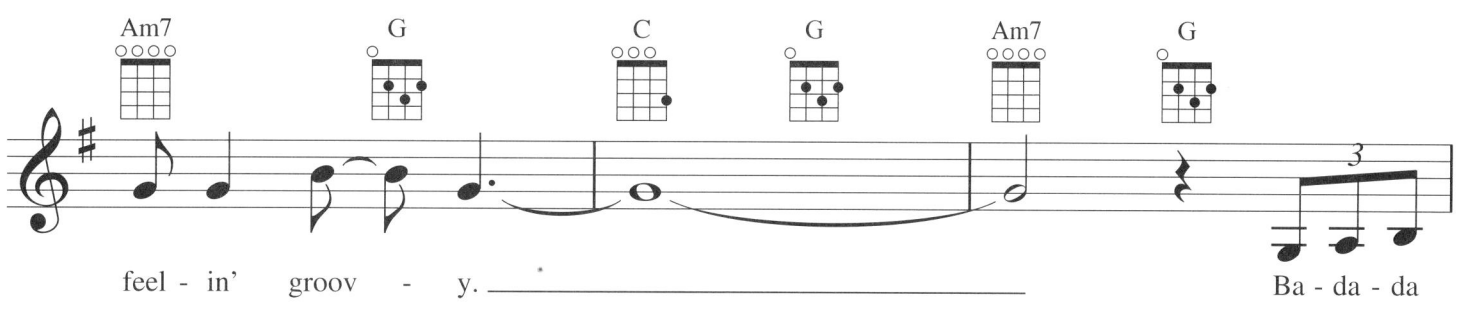
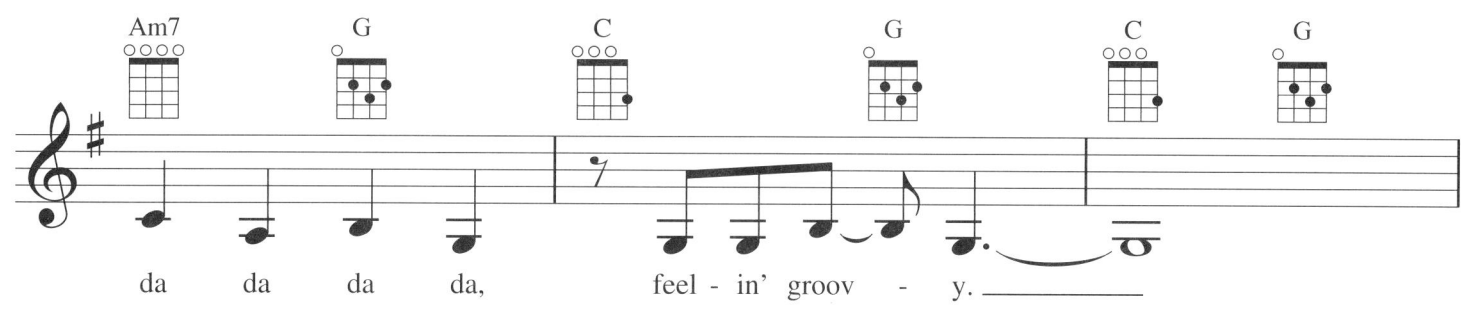

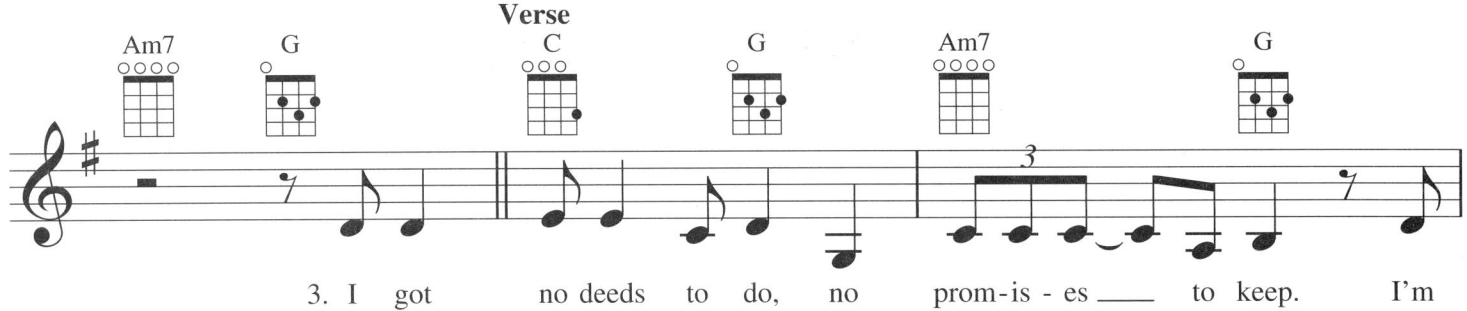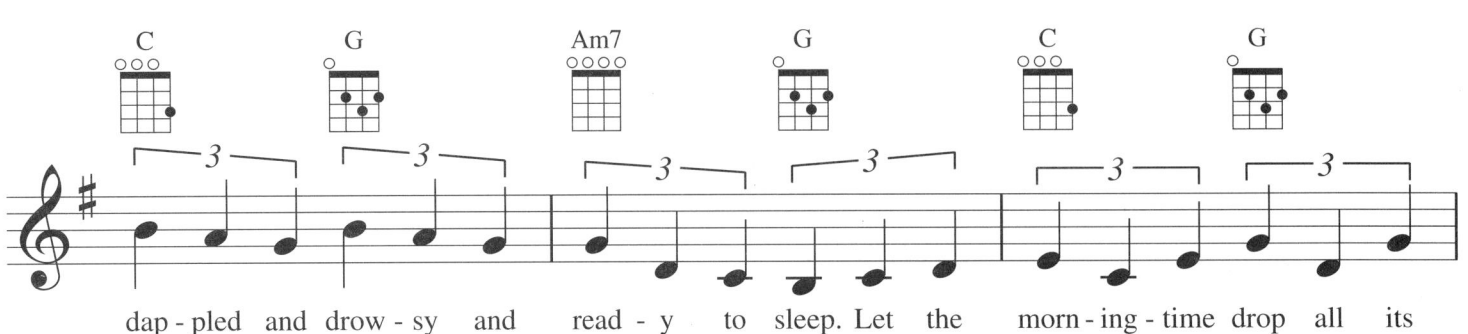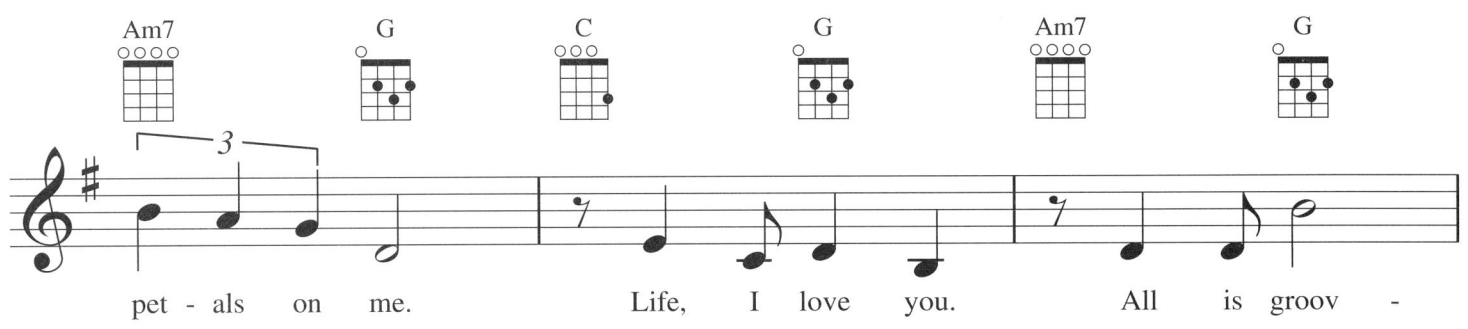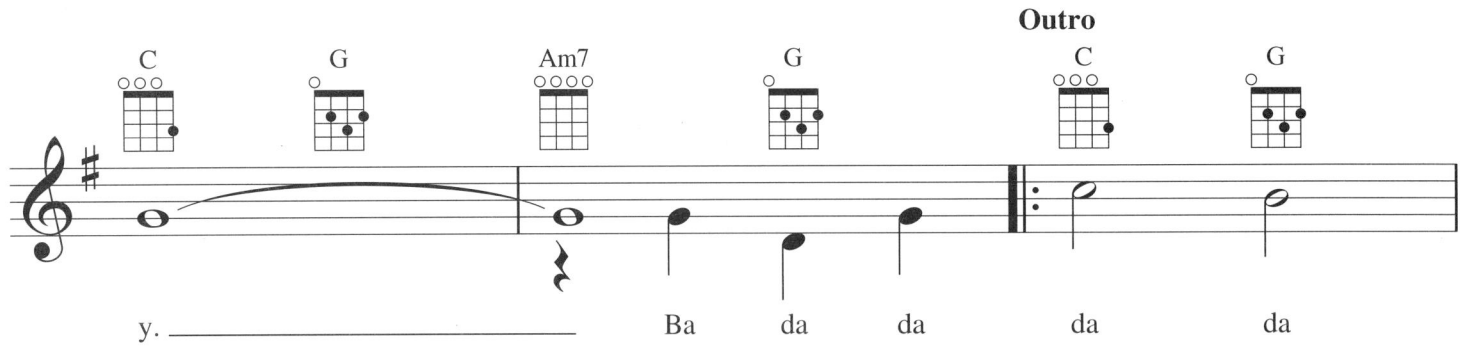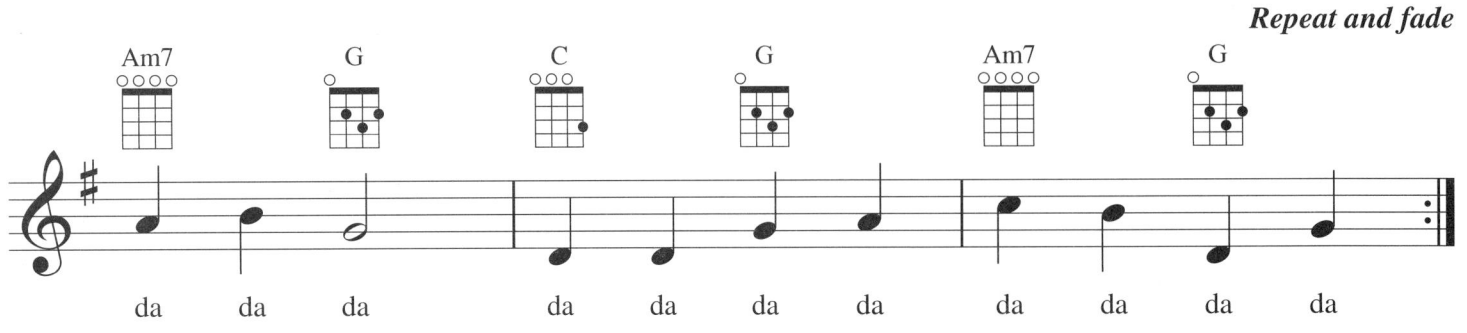

Greenback Dollar

Words and Music by Hoyt Axton and Ken Ramsey

1. Some people say I'm a no-'count;
2. When I was a little babe
3. Now that I'm a grown man, I've

others say I'm no good. But
my mama said, "Hey, son,
trav-eled here and there. I've

I'm just a nat-'ral-born trav-el-in' man
trav-el where you will and grow to be a man, and
learned that a bot-tle of bran-dy and a song, the

Copyright © 1962 IRVING MUSIC, INC.
Copyright Renewed
All Rights Reserved Used by Permission

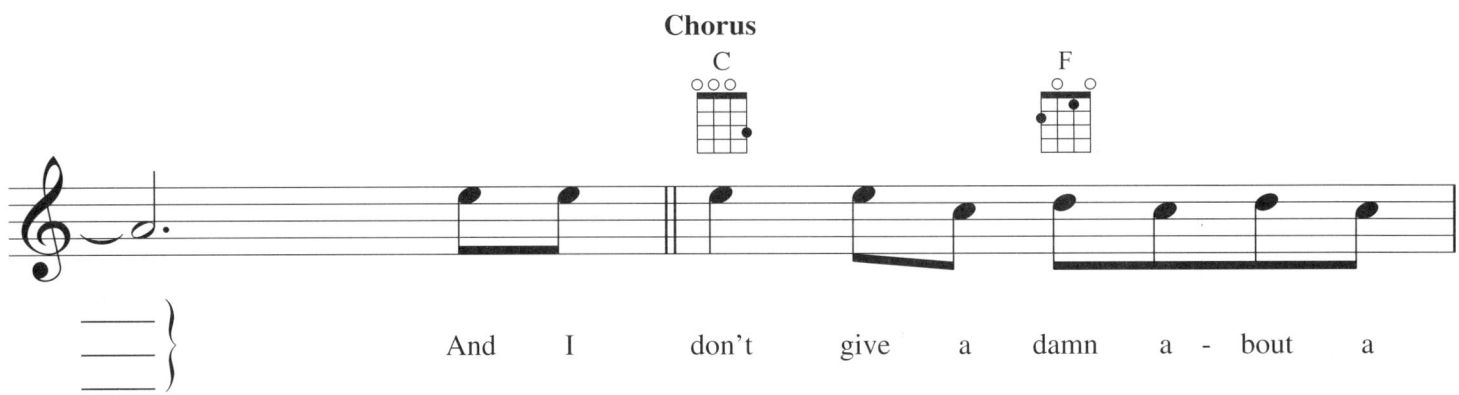
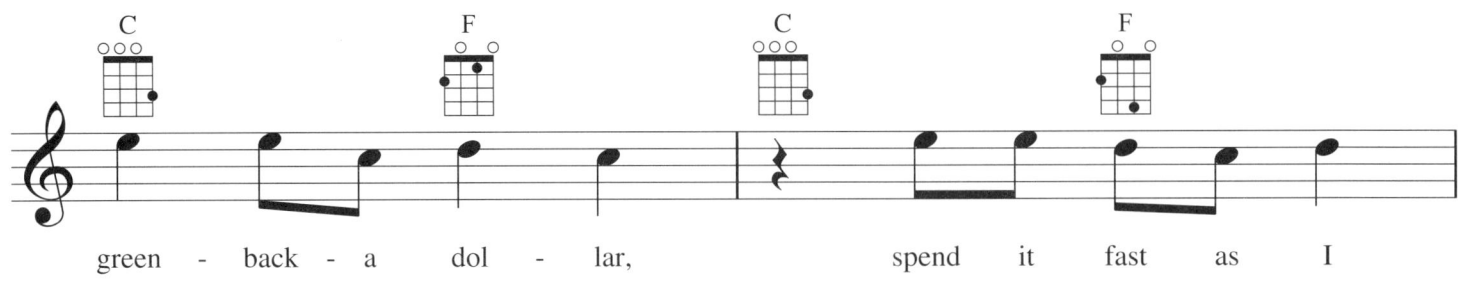
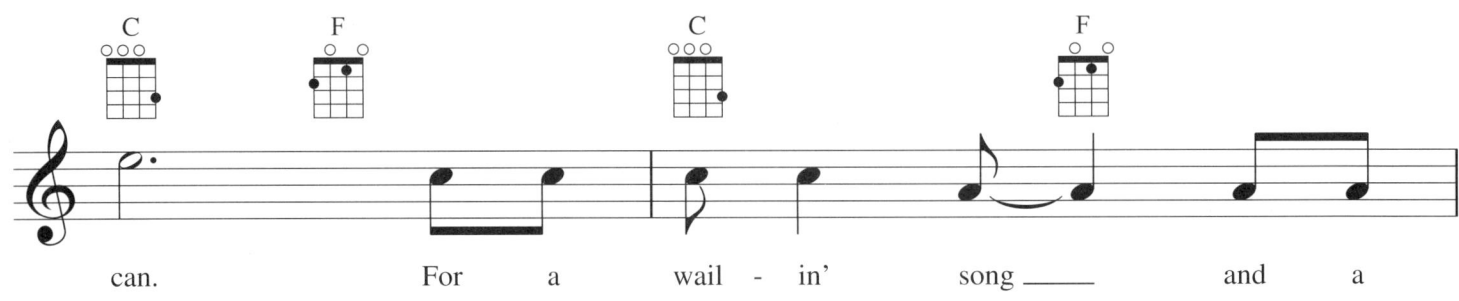

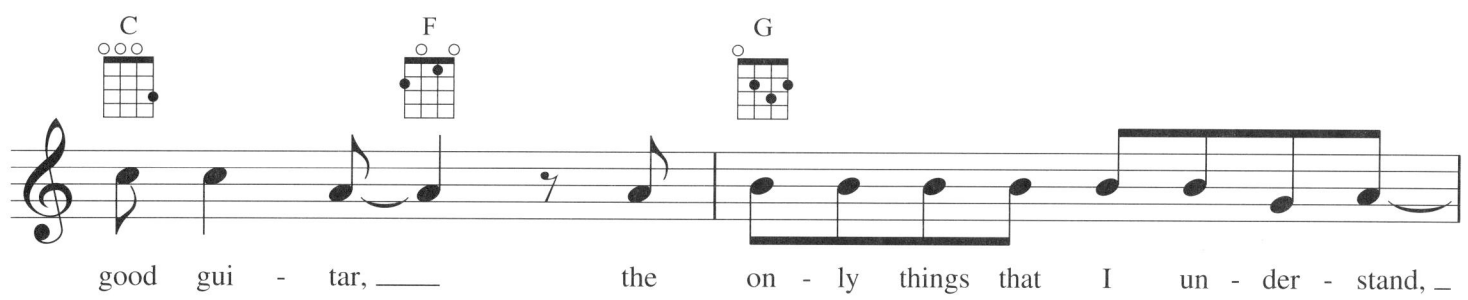
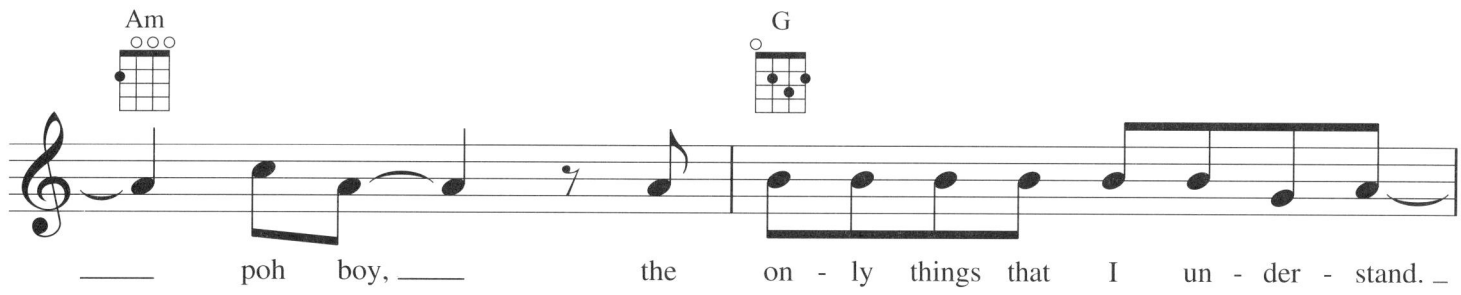

Green Green Grass of Home

Words and Music by Curly Putman

First note
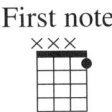

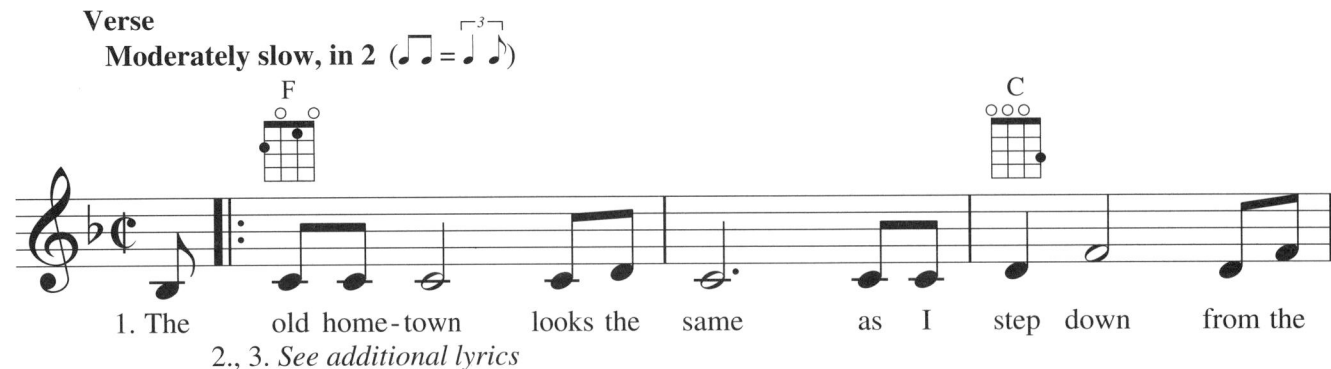

1. The old home-town looks the same as I step down from the
2., 3. *See additional lyrics*

train, and there to meet me is my ma-ma and

pa-pa. Down the road I look, and there runs Mar-y,

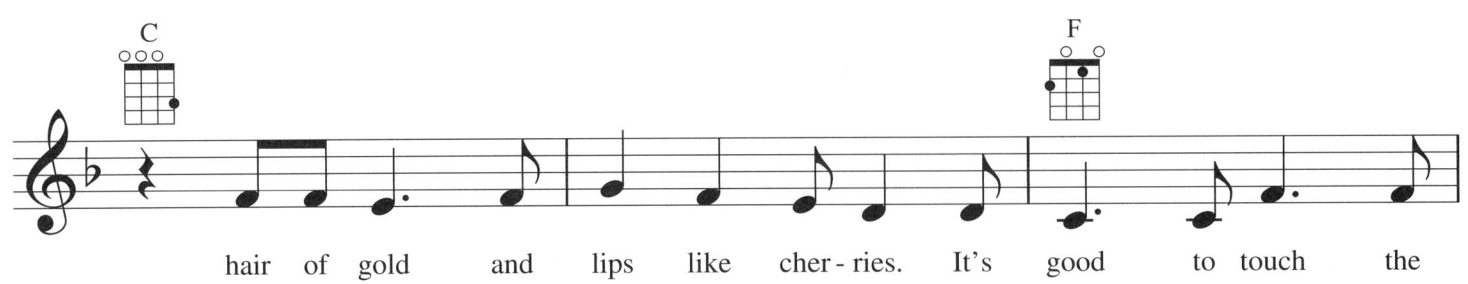

hair of gold and lips like cher-ries. It's good to touch the

Copyright © 1965 Sony/ATV Music Publishing LLC
Copyright Renewed
All Rights Administered by Sony/ATV Music Publishing LLC, 8 Music Square West, Nashville, TN 37203
International Copyright Secured   All Rights Reserved

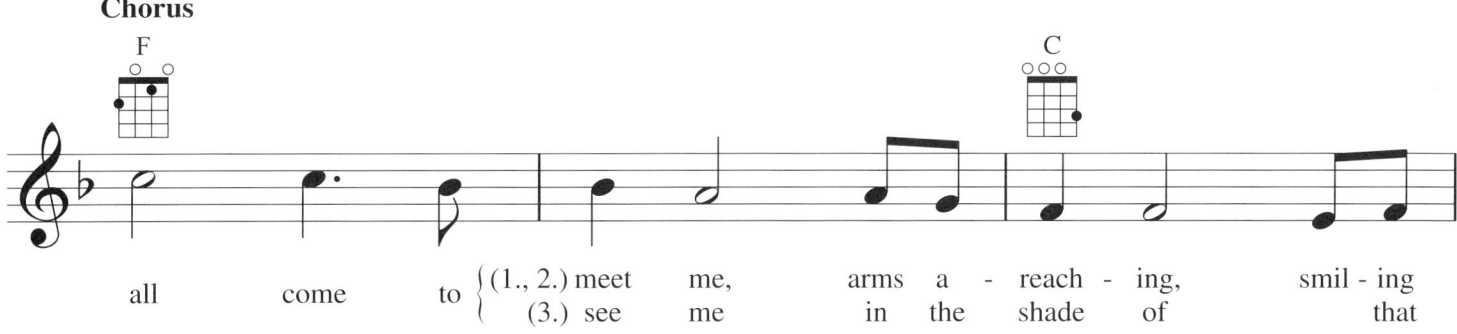

Additional Lyrics

2. The old house is still standing, though the paint is cracked and dry.
   And there's that old oak tree that I used to play on.
   Down the lane I walk with my sweet Mary, hair of gold and lips like cherries.
   It's good to touch the green, green grass of home.

3. *(Spoken:) Then I awake, and look around me at four gray walls that surround me,
   And I realize that I was only dreaming.
   For there's a guard and there's a sad, old padre. Arm in arm we'll walk at daybreak.
   Again I'll touch the green, green grass of home.*

Greenfields

Words and Music by Terry Gilkyson,
Richard Dehr and Frank Miller

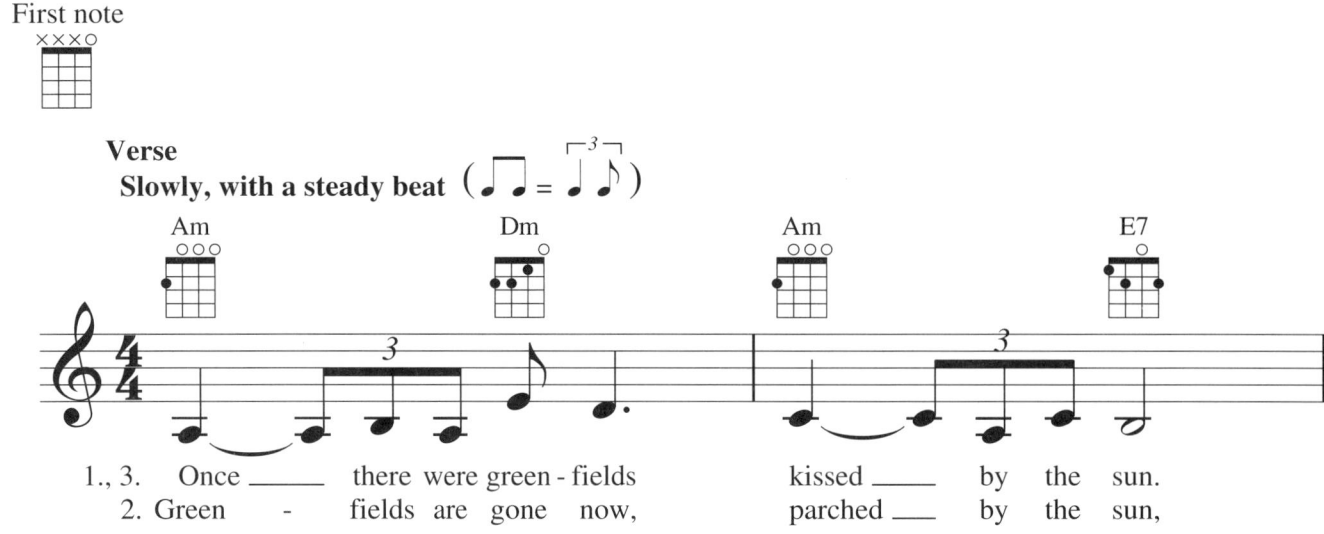

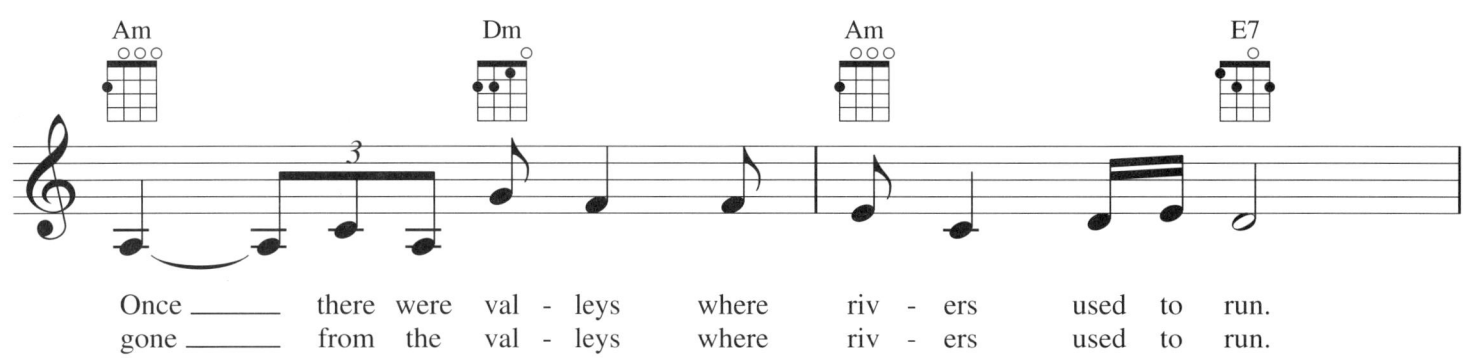

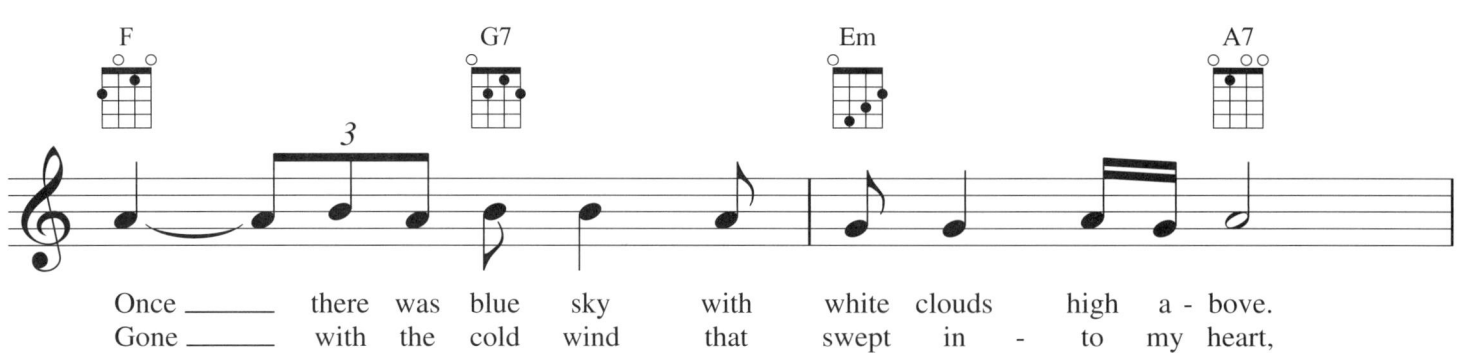

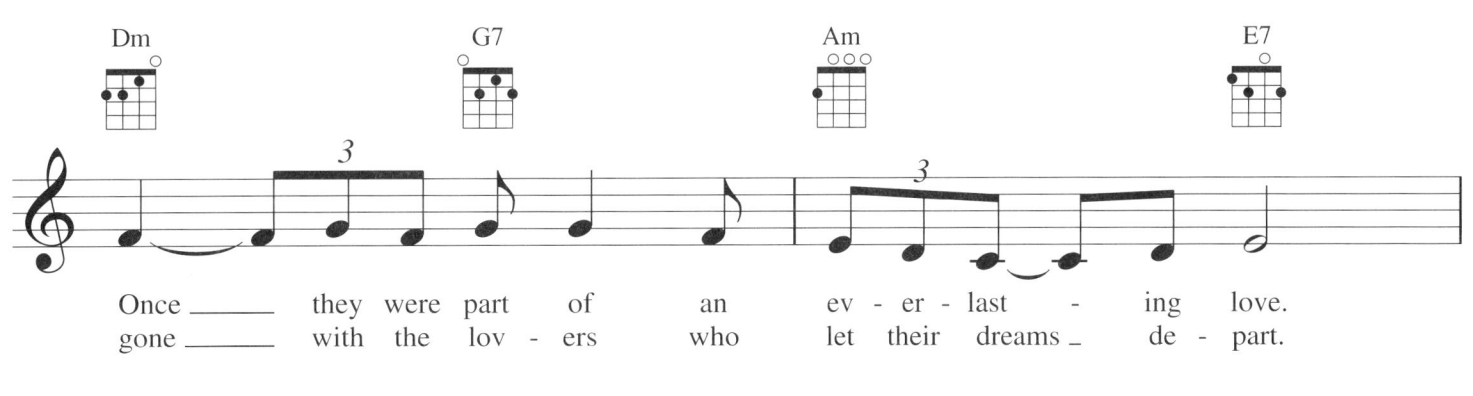
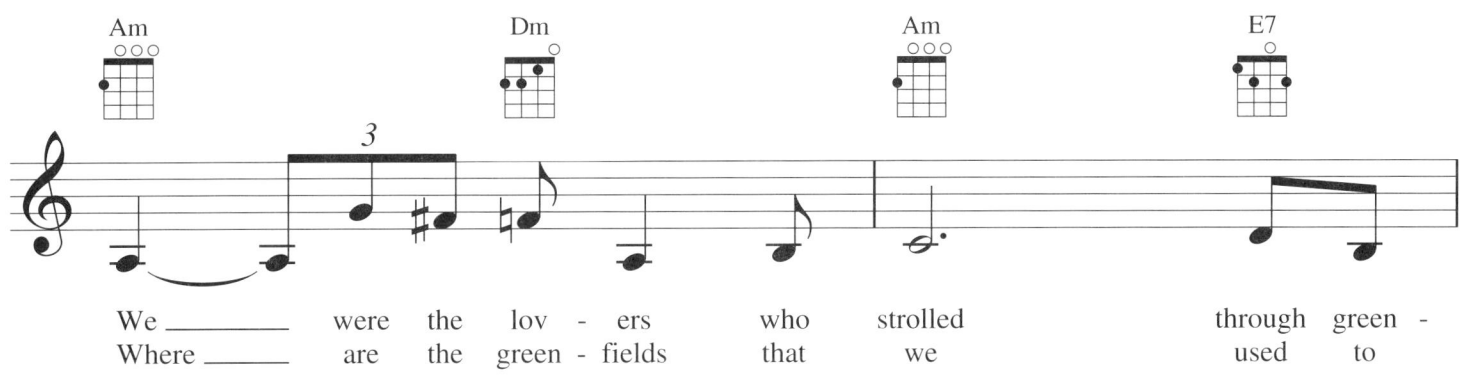
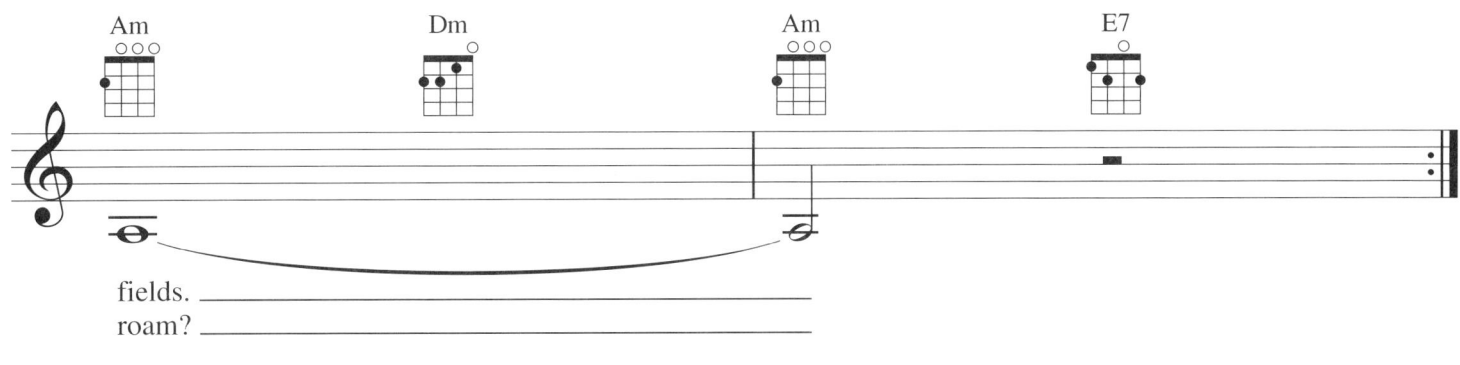
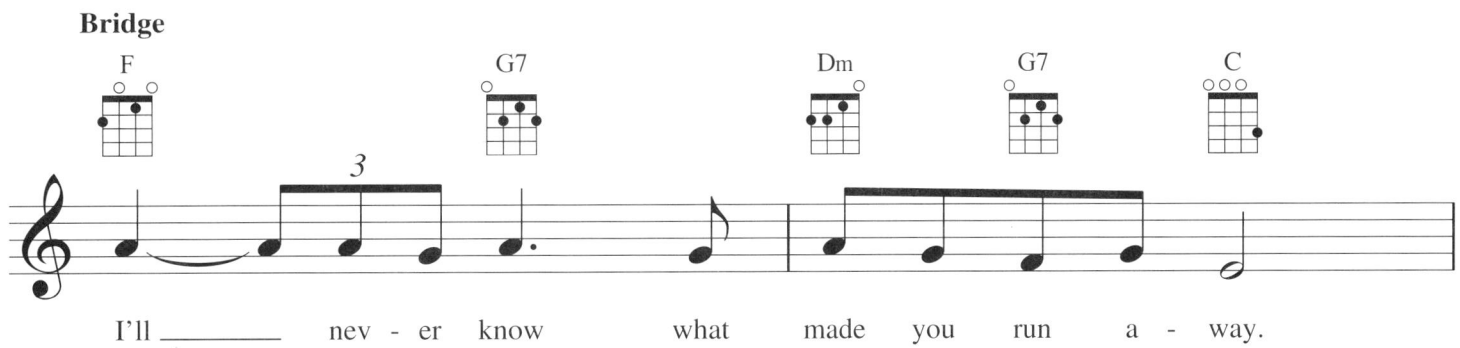
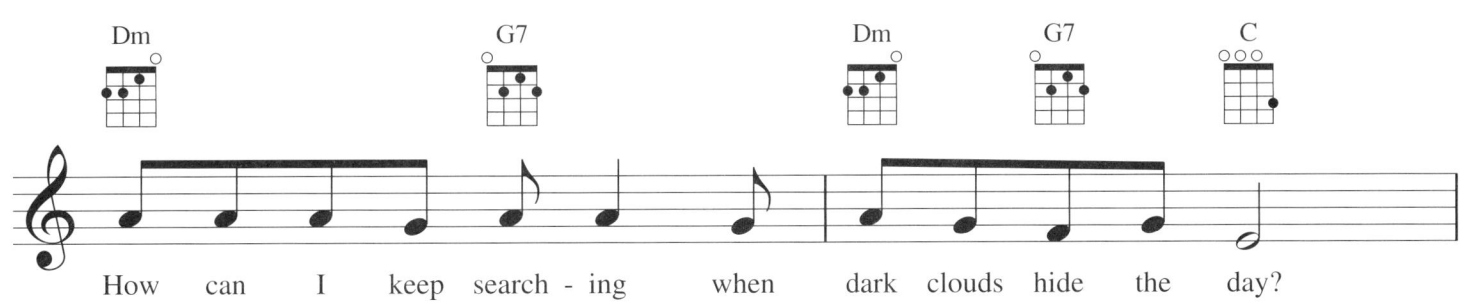

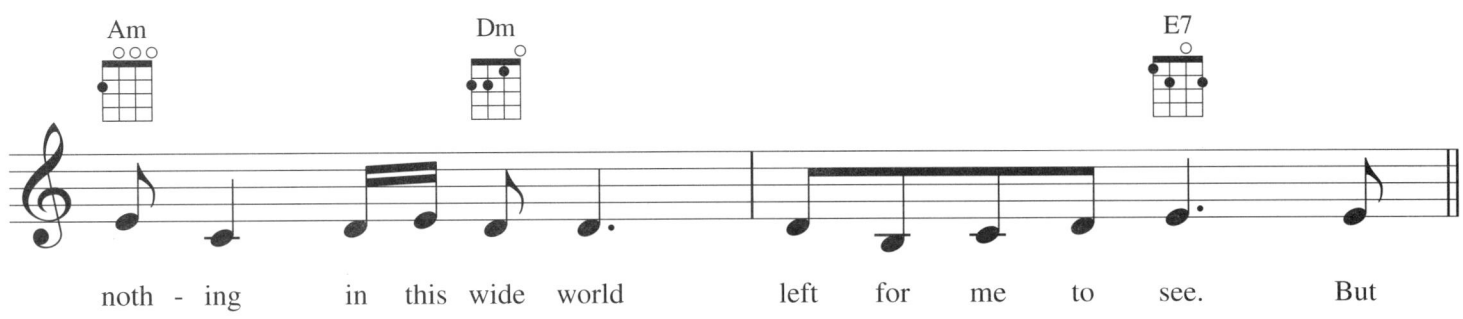

Chorus

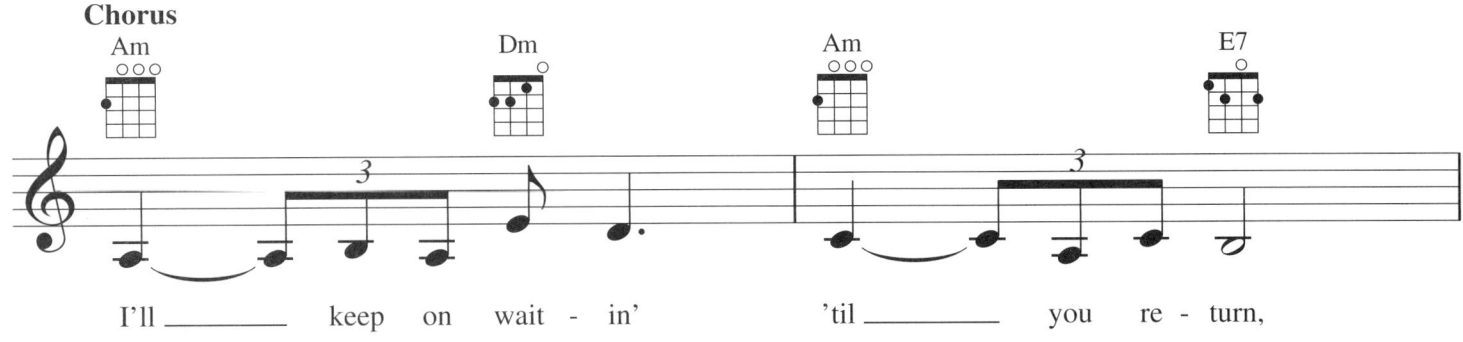

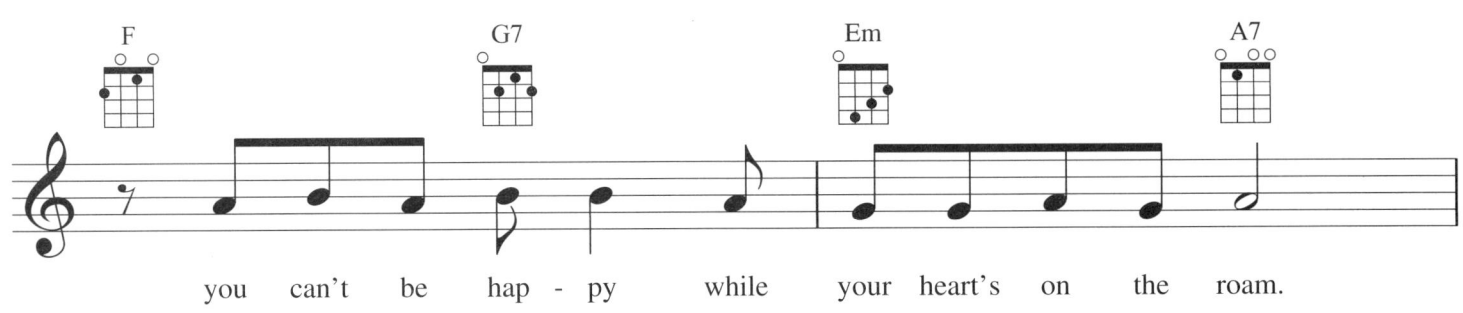

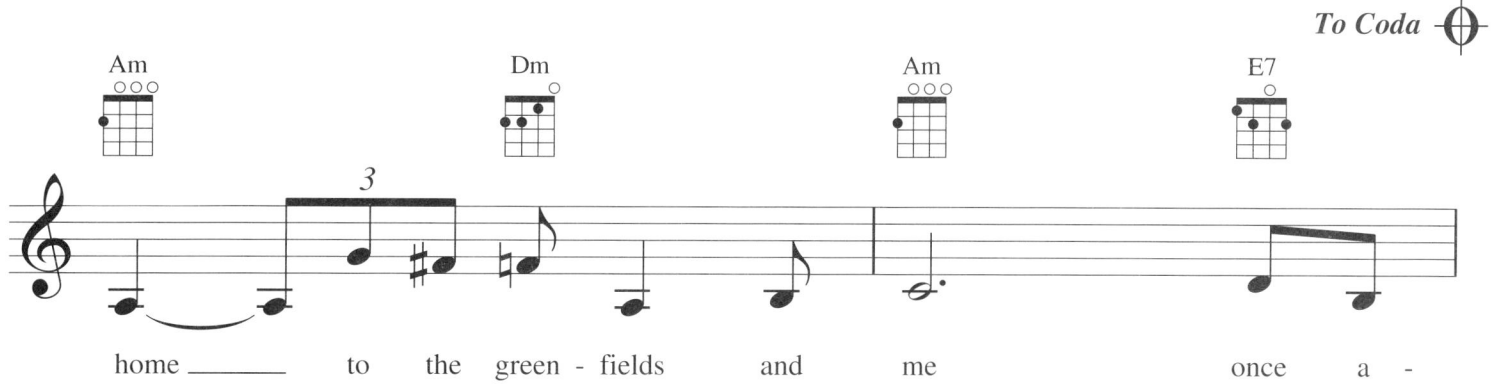
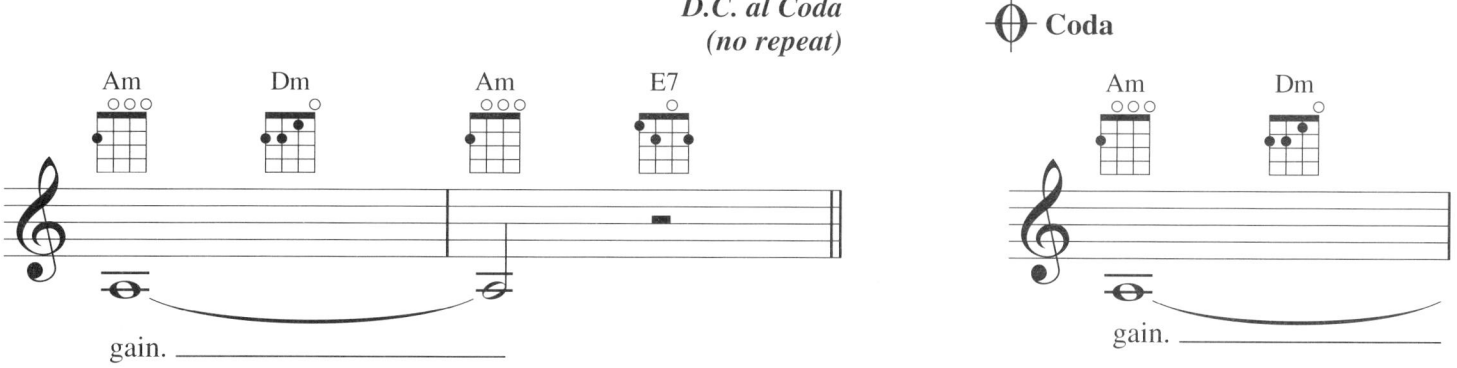
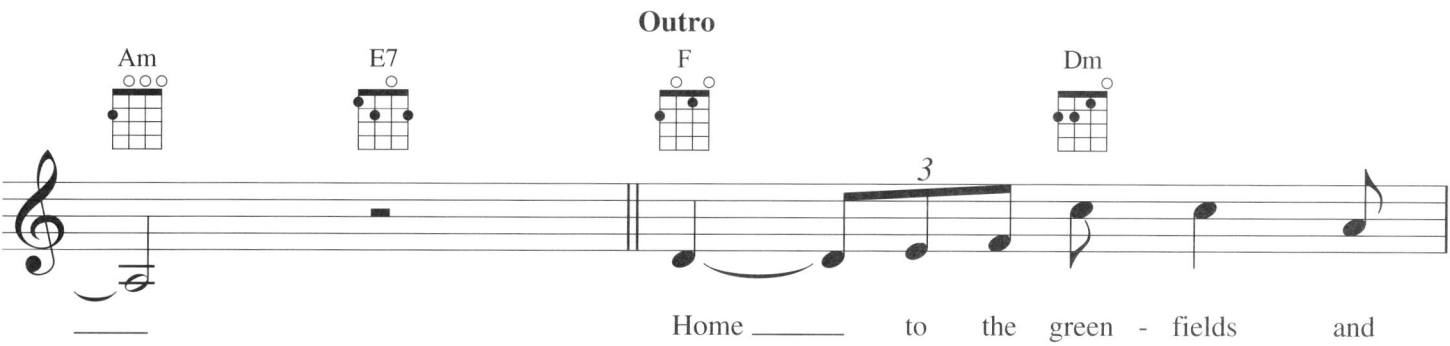
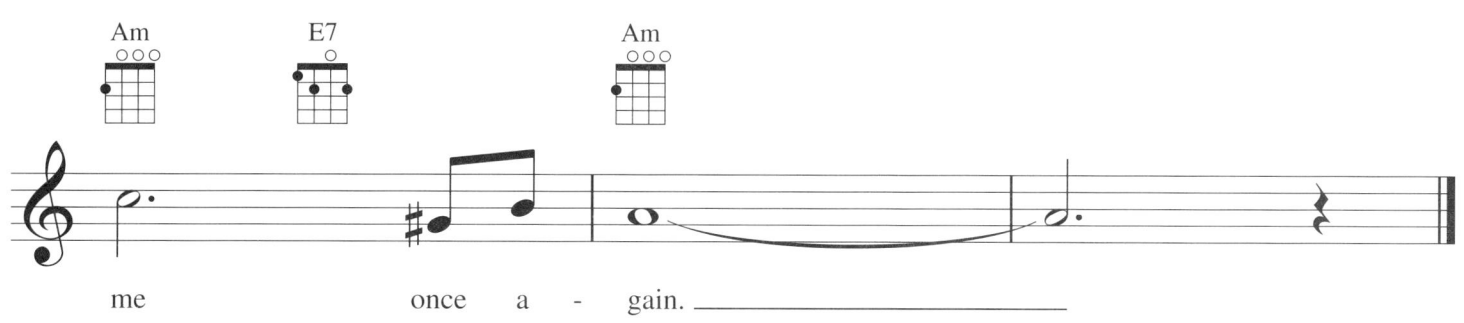

Guantanamera

Cuban Folksong

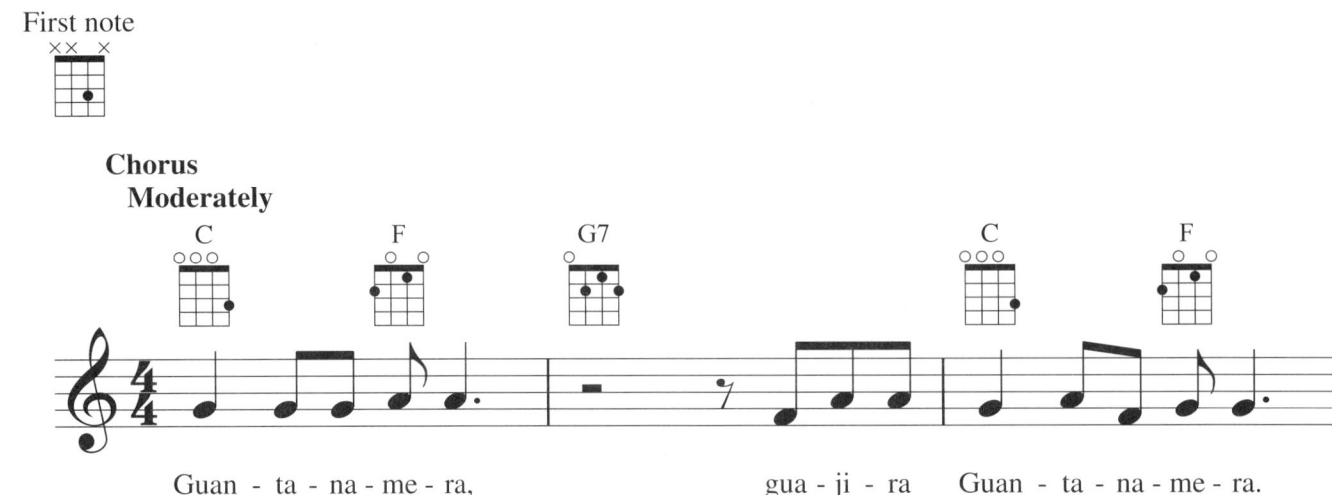
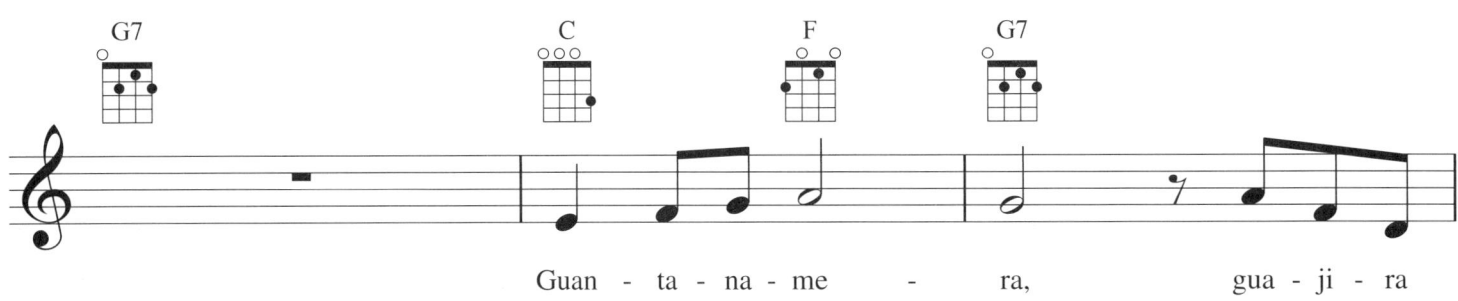

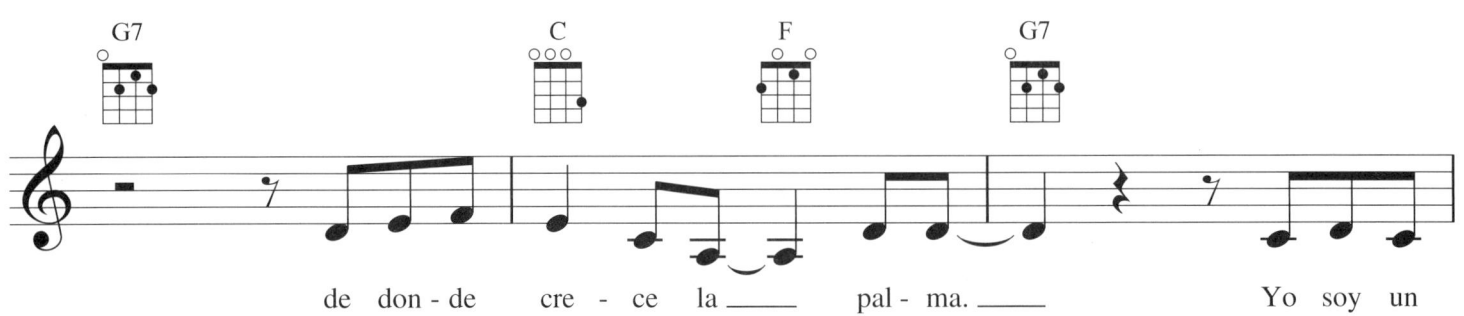

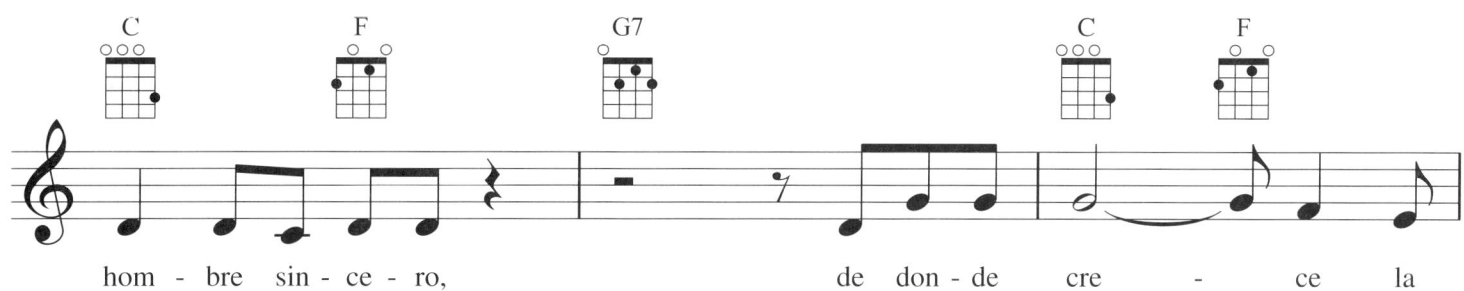
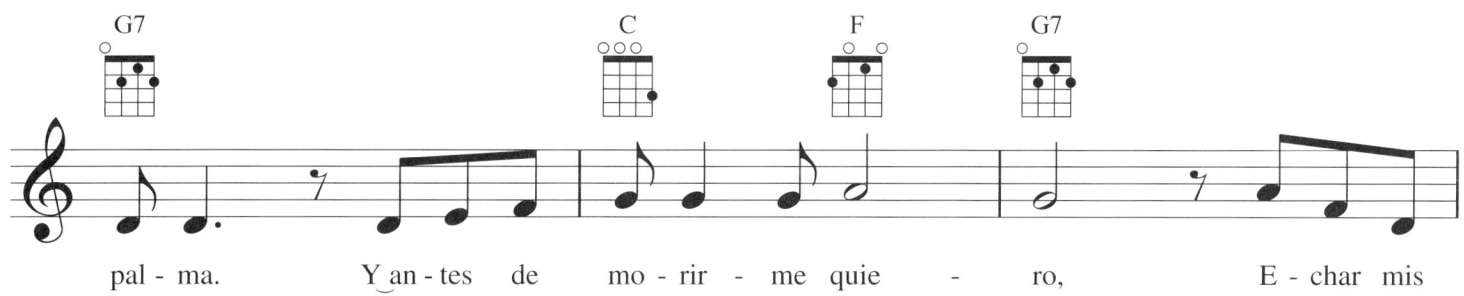
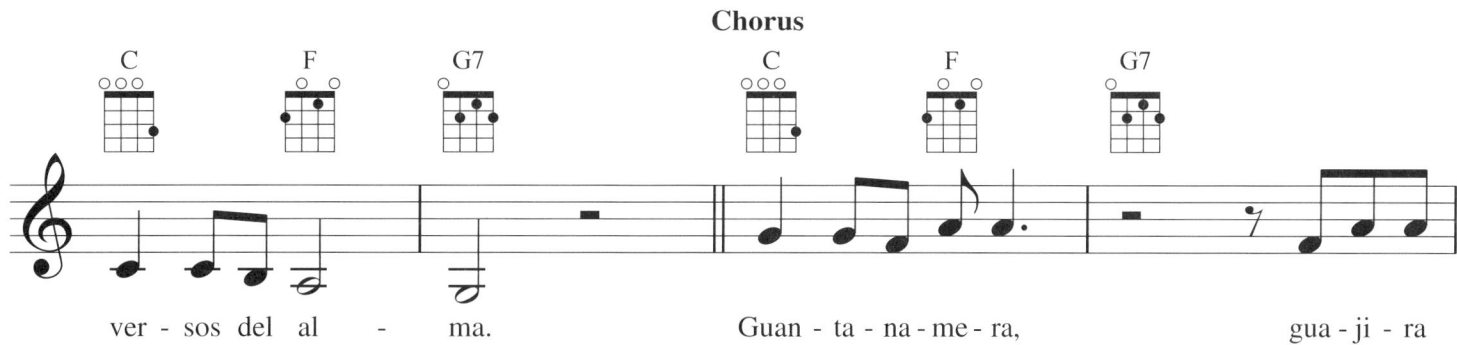
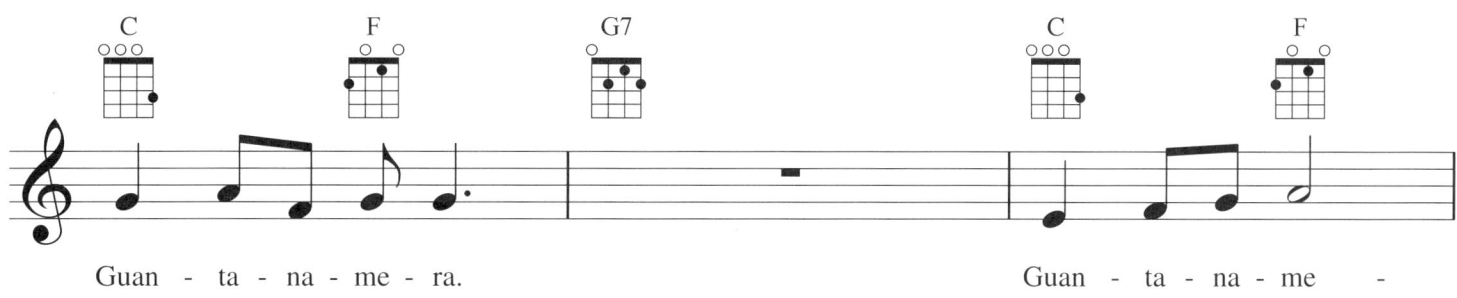

The House of the Rising Sun

Words and Music by Alan Price

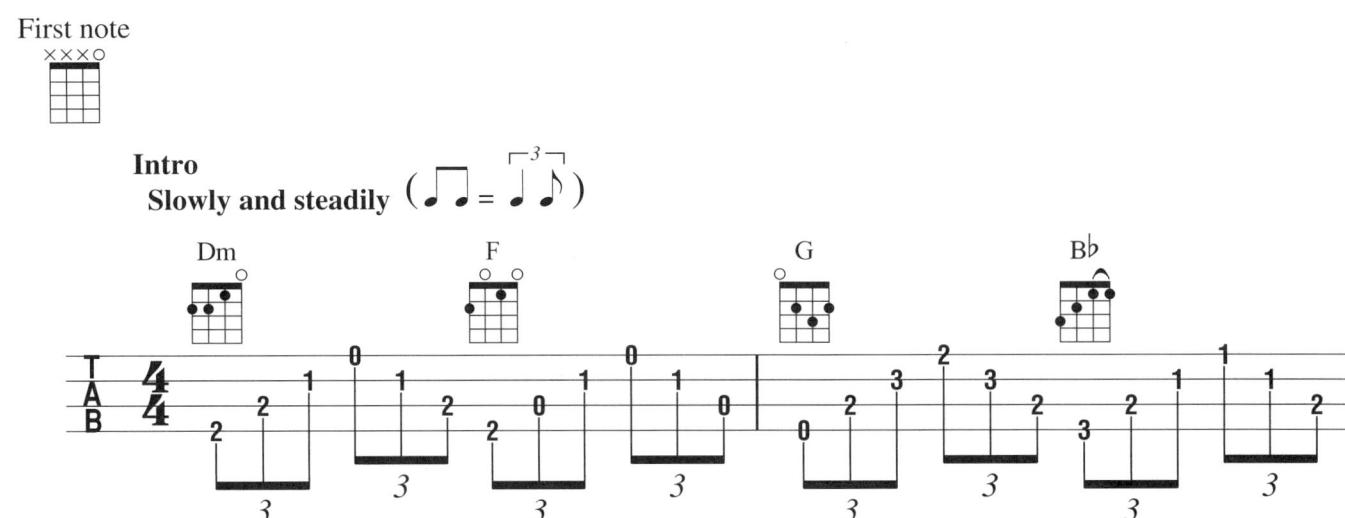

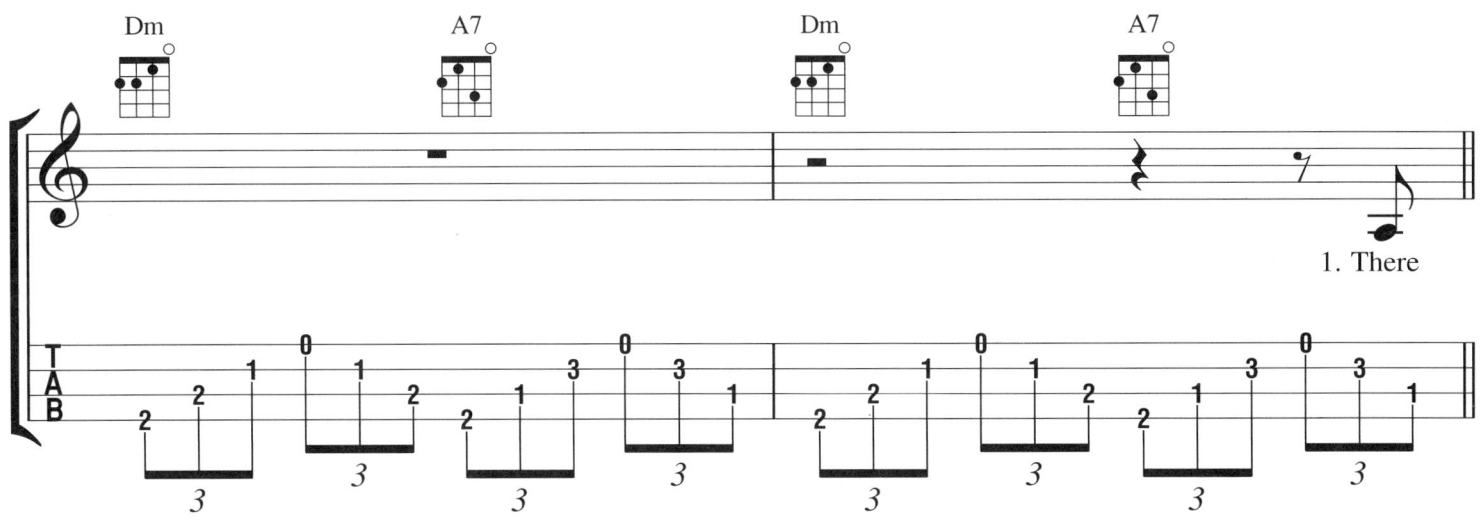

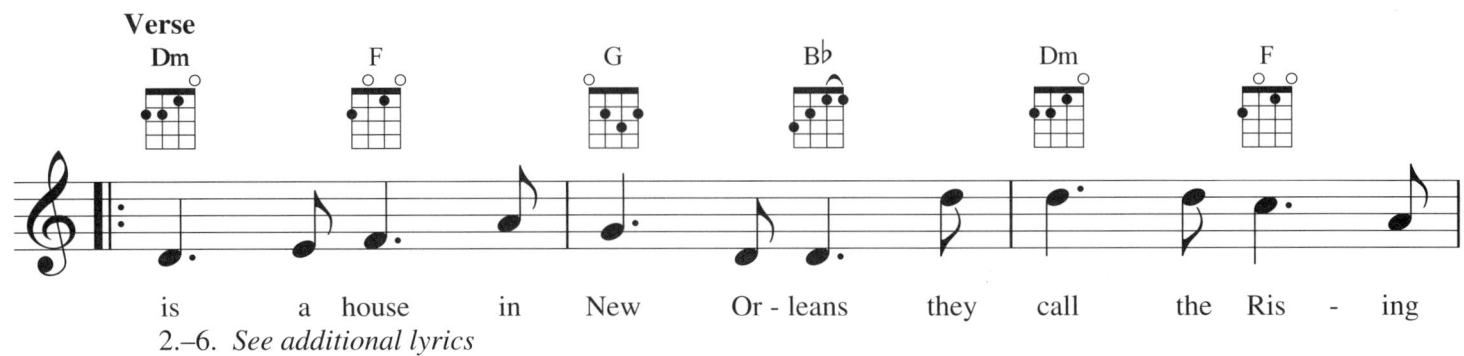

2.–6. *See additional lyrics*

© 1964 (Renewed 1992) KEITH PROWSE MUSIC PUBLISHING CO., LTD.
All Rights Reserved   International Copyright Secured   Used by Permission

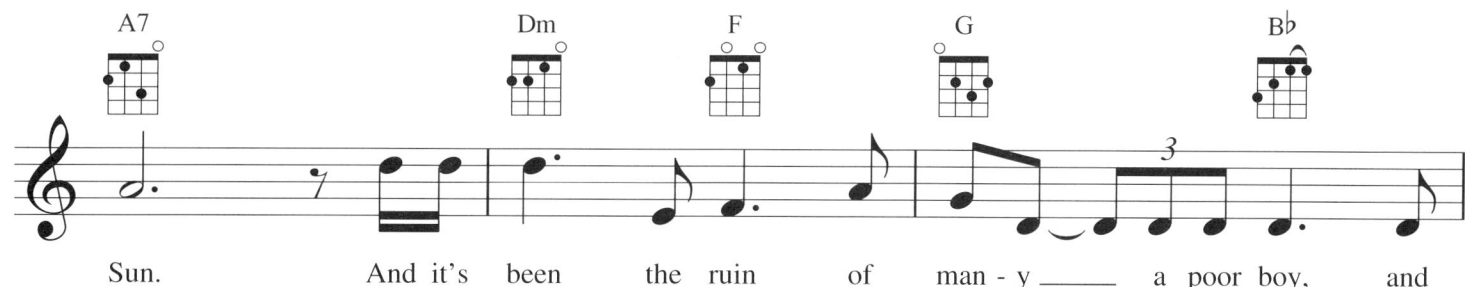

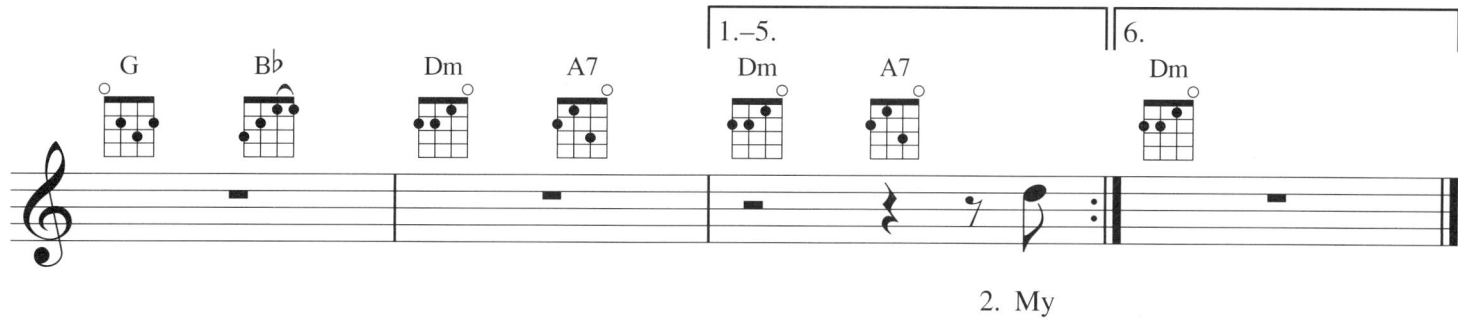

Additional Lyrics

2. My mother was a tailor, sewed my new blue jeans.
   My father was a gamblin' man down in New Orleans.

3. Now, the only thing a gambler needs is a suitcase and a trunk.
   And the only time he'll be satisfied is when he's all a-drunk.

4. Oh! mother, tell your children not to do what I have done:
   Spend your lives in sin and misery in the House of the Rising Sun.

5. Well, I've got one foot on the platform, the other foot on the train.
   I'm going back to New Orleans to wear that ball and chain.

6. Well, there is a house in New Orleans they call the Rising Sun.
   And it's been the ruin of many a poor boy, and God, I know I'm one.

Lemon Tree

Words and Music by Will Holt

First note
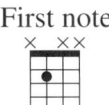

Verse
Moderately

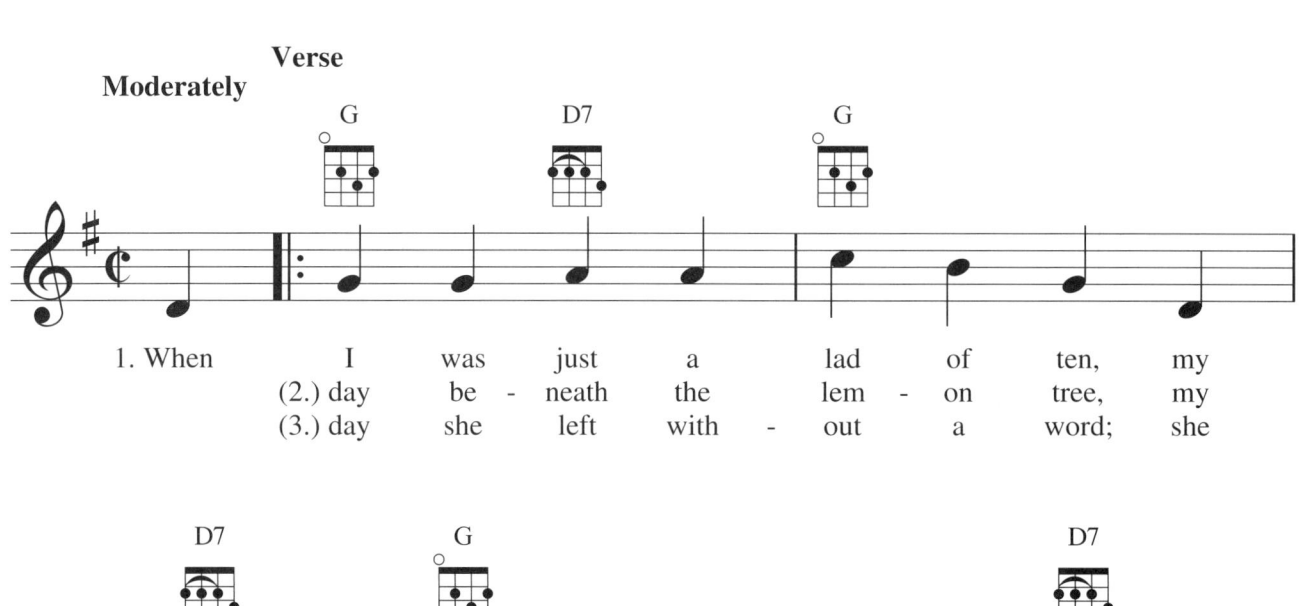

1. When I was just a lad of ten, my
(2.) day be-neath the lem-on tree, my
(3.) day she left with-out a word; she

fa-ther said to me, "Come here and take a
love and I did lie, a girl so sweet that
took a-way the sun. And in the dark she

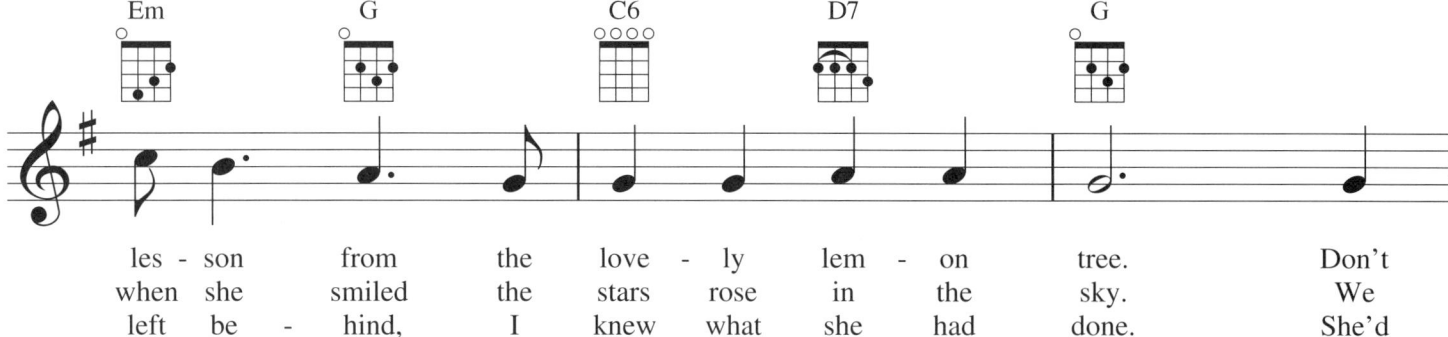

les-son from the love-ly lem-on tree. Don't
when she smiled the stars rose in the sky. We
left be-hind, I knew what she had done. She'd

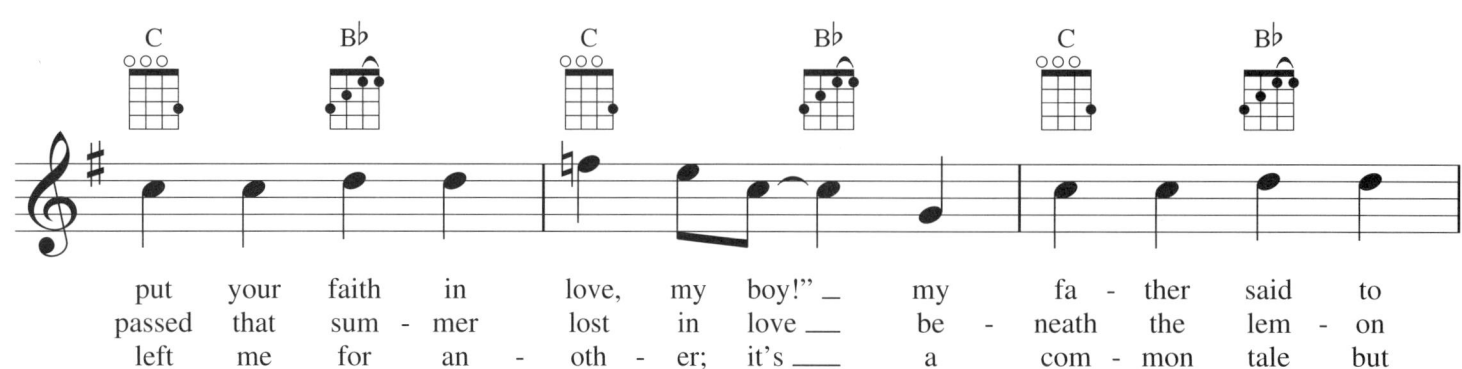

put your faith in love, my boy!" my fa-ther said to
passed that sum-mer lost in love be-neath the lem-on
left me for an-oth-er; it's a com-mon tale but

Copyright © 1960 (Renewed) by Wise Brothers Music, LLC (ASCAP)
International Copyright Secured All Rights Reserved
Reprinted by Permission

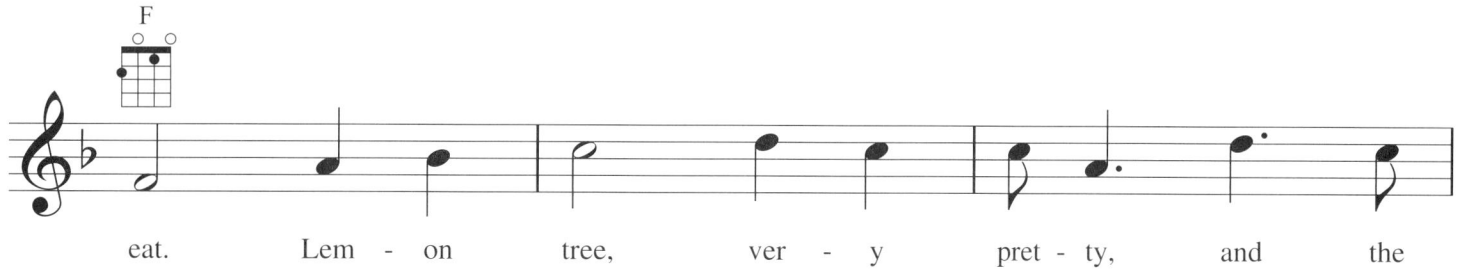

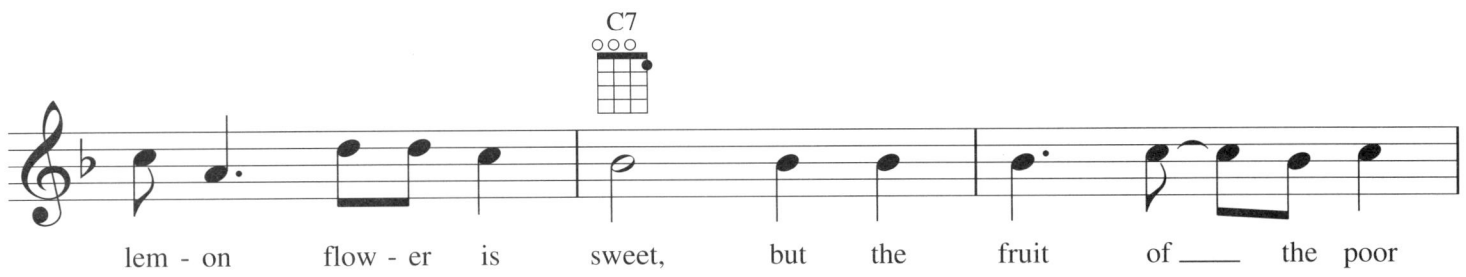
lem - on flow - er is sweet, but the fruit of ___ the poor

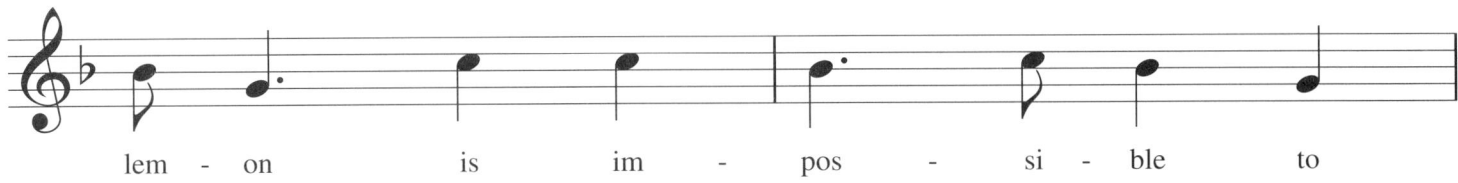
lem - on is im - pos - si - ble to

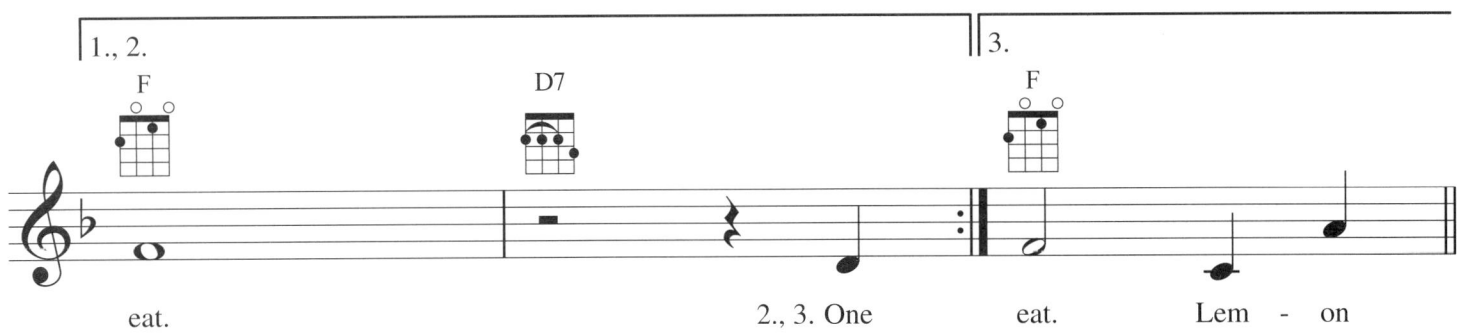
eat.   2., 3. One eat. Lem - on

Outro

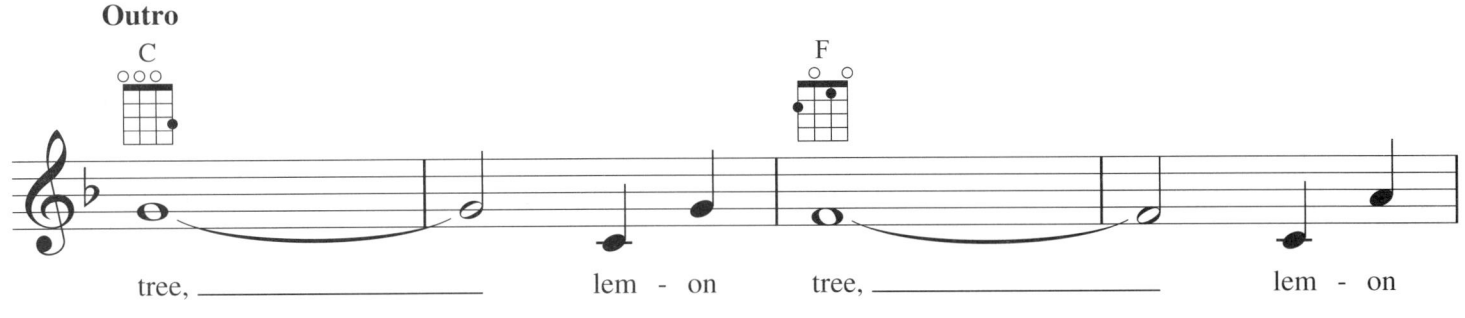
tree, ___ lem - on tree, ___ lem - on

tree, ___ lem - on tree.

Midnight Special

Words and Music by John Fogerty

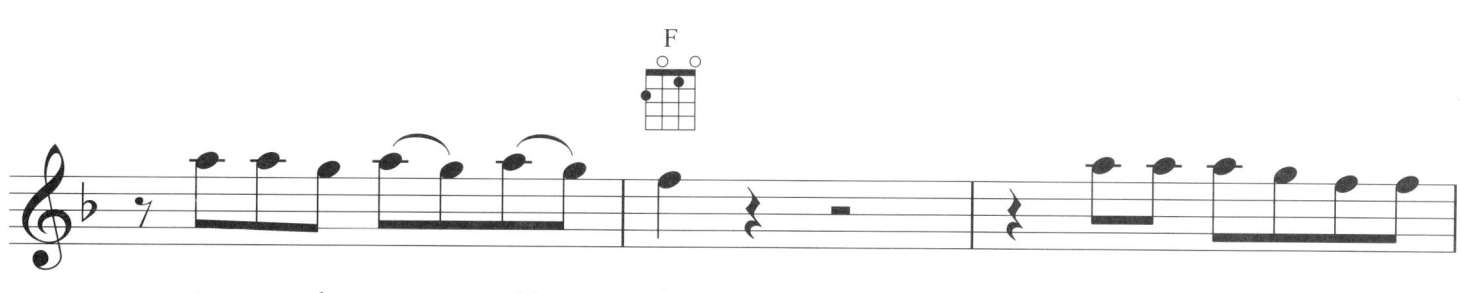

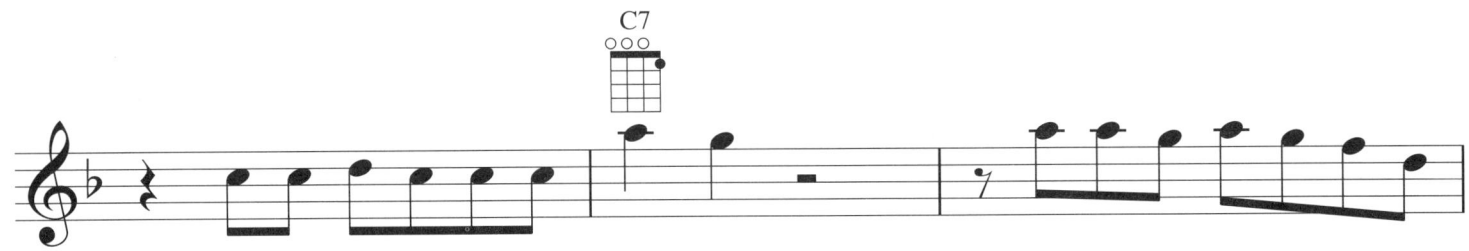

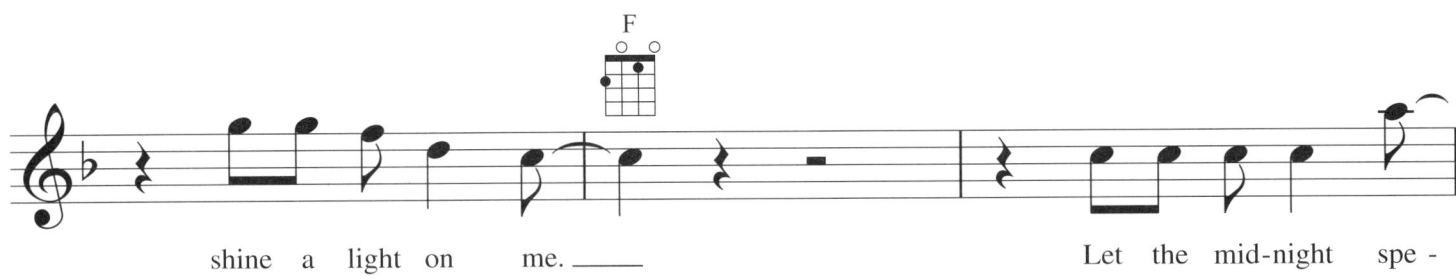

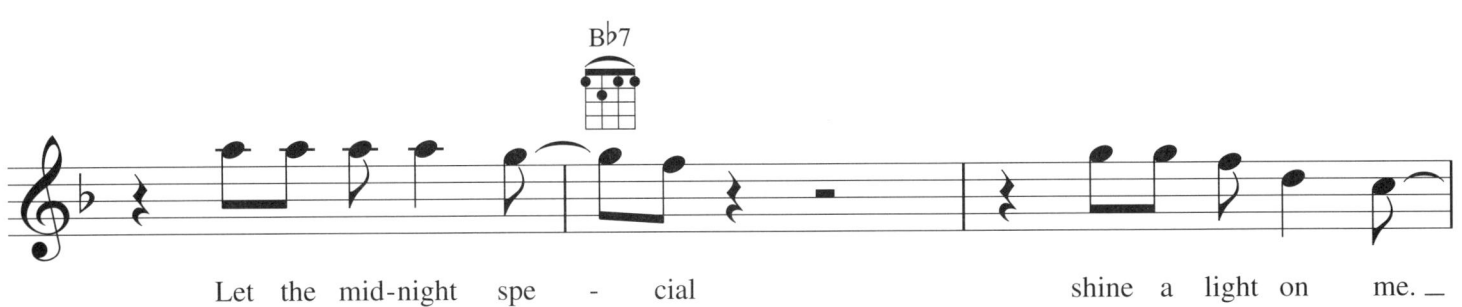

38

Let the mid-night spe-cial

To Coda ⊕

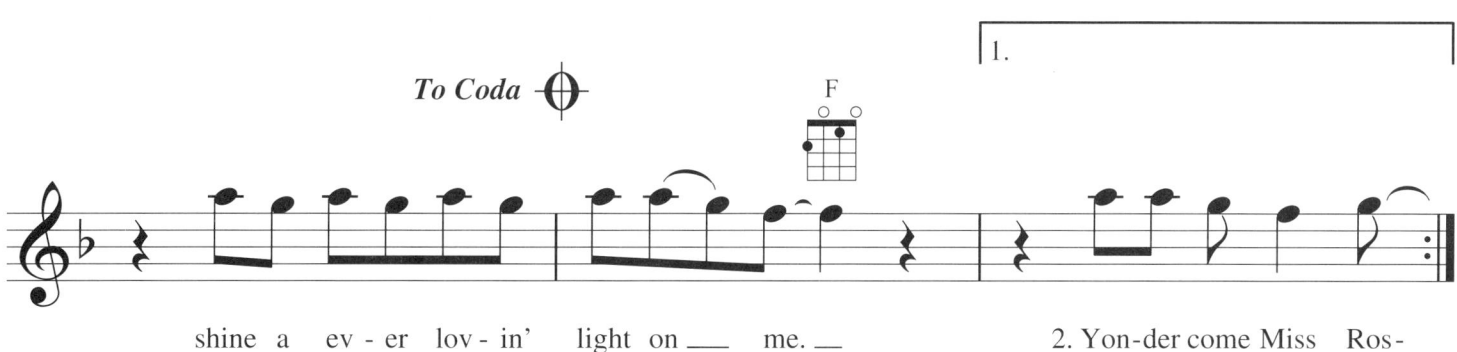

shine a ev-er lov-in' light on ___ me. ___   2. Yon-der come Miss Ros-

D.S. al Coda

⊕ Coda

3. If you're ev-er in   light on ___ me. ___

Additional Lyrics

2. Yonder come Miss Rosie.
   How in the world did you know?
   By the way she wears her apron
   And the clothes she wore.
   Umbrella on her shoulder,
   Piece of paper in her hand.
   She come to see the Governor;
   She wants to free her man.

3. If you're ever in Houston,
   Well, you better do right.
   You better not gamble;
   You better not fight.
   Or the sheriff will grab ya,
   And the boys will bring you down.
   The next thing you know, boy,
   Oh, you're prison-bound.

The M.T.A.
Words and Music by Jacqueline Steiner and Bess Hawes

40

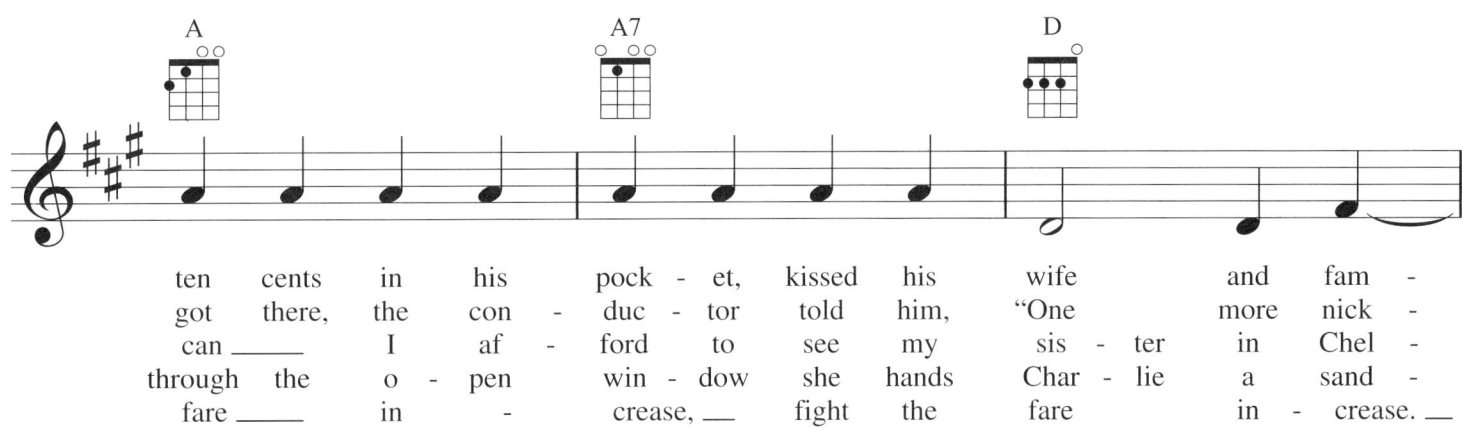
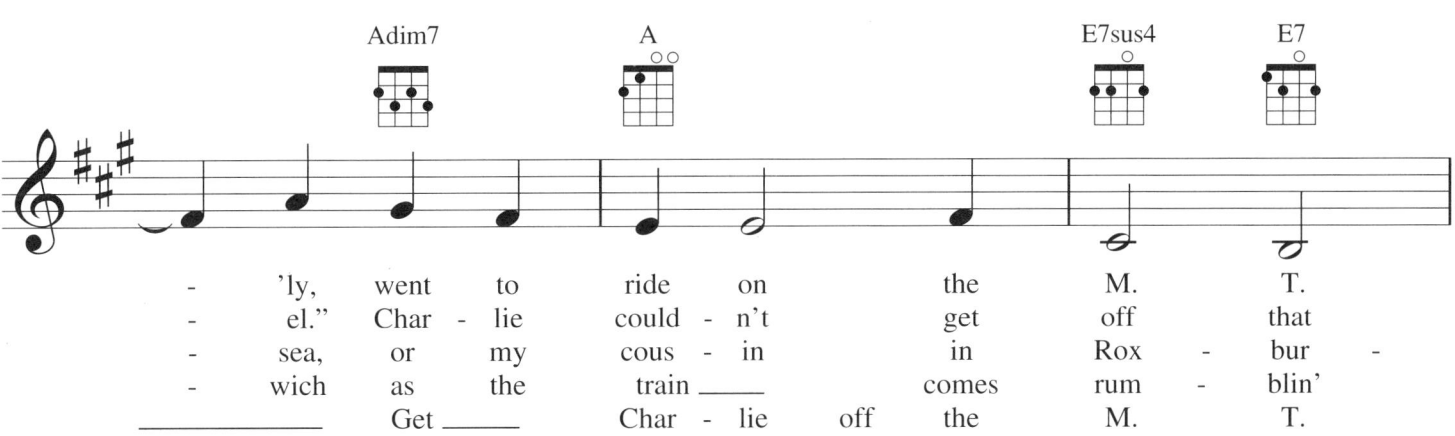
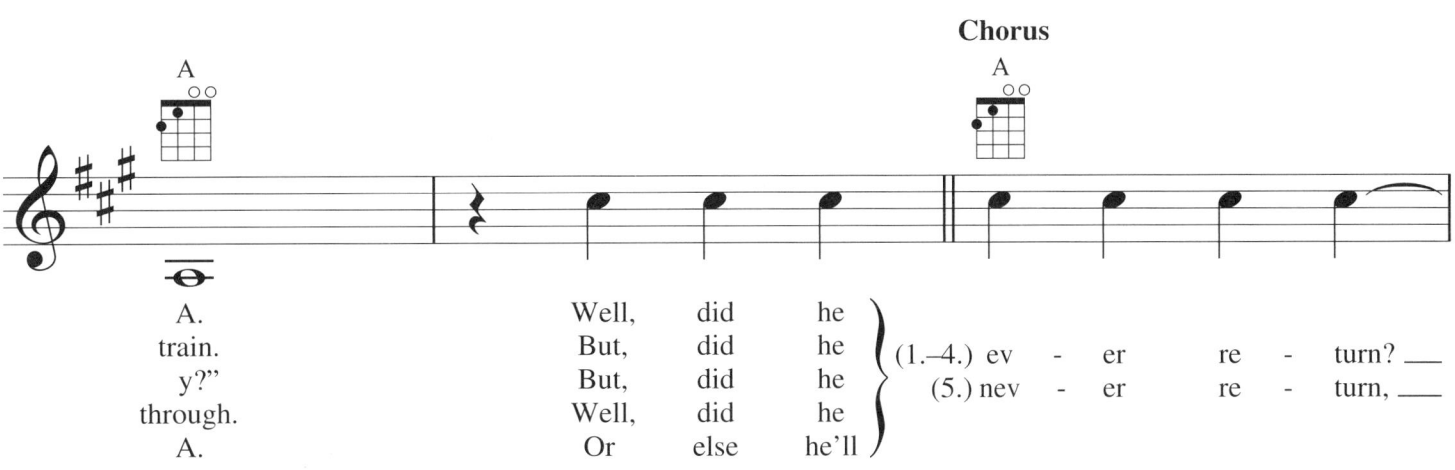
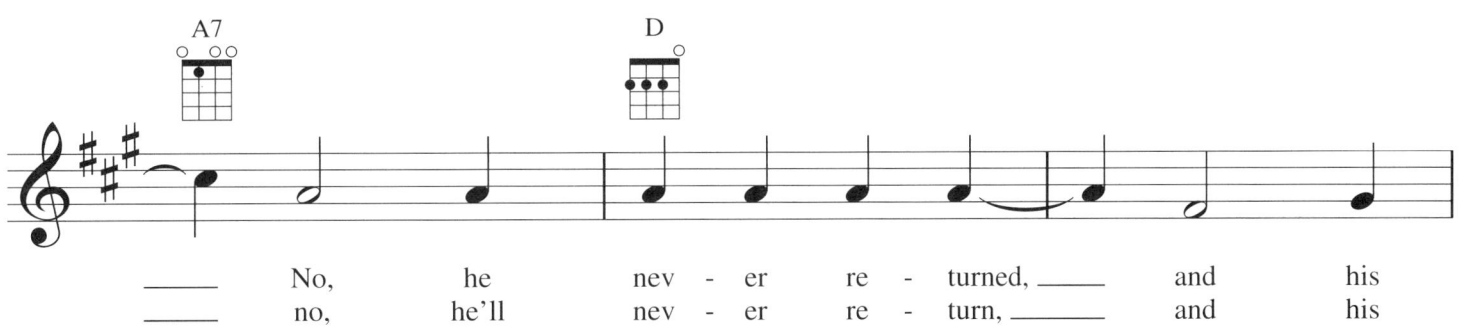

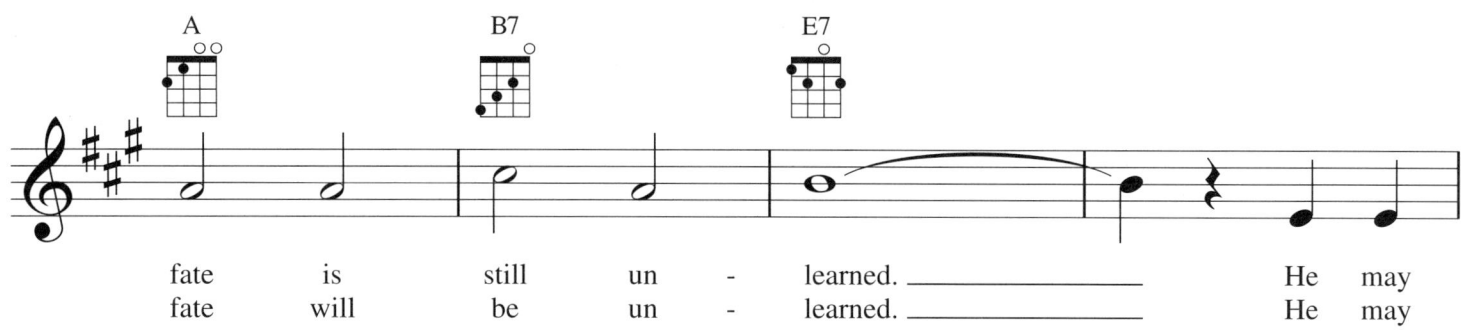
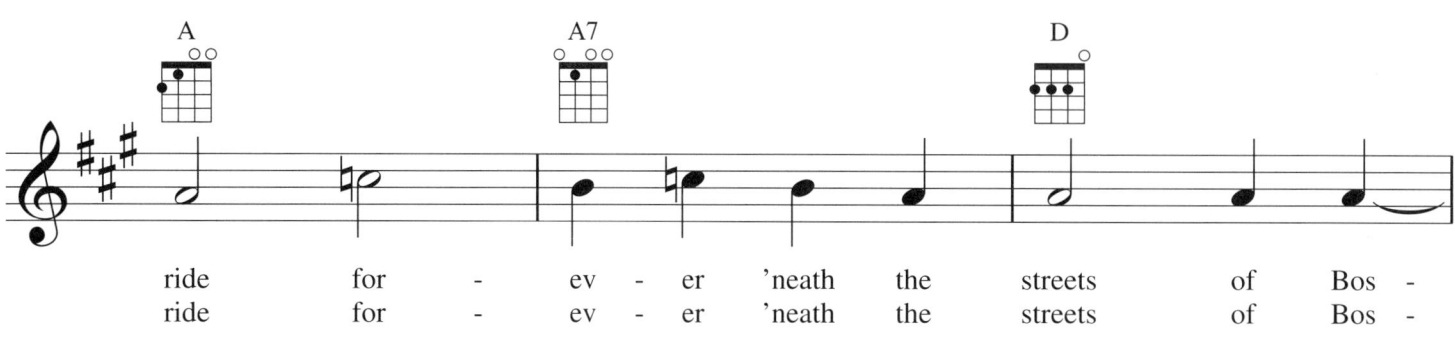
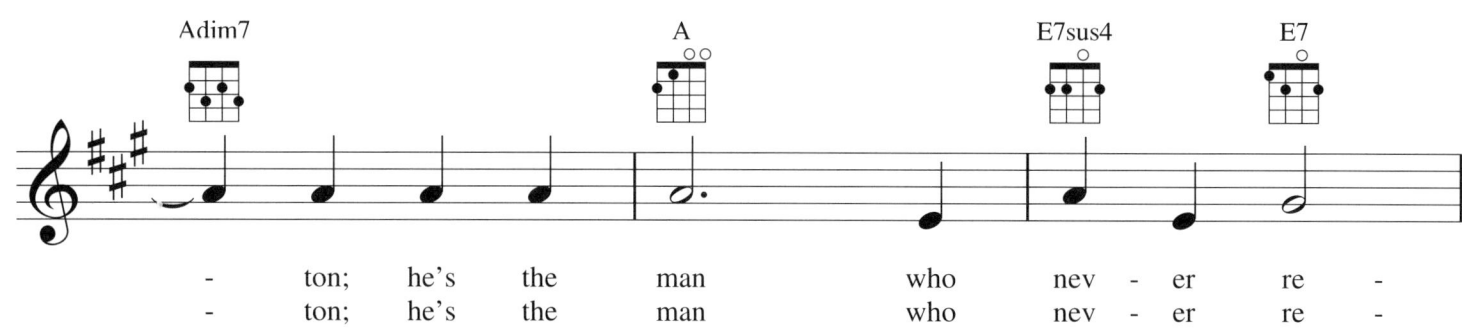
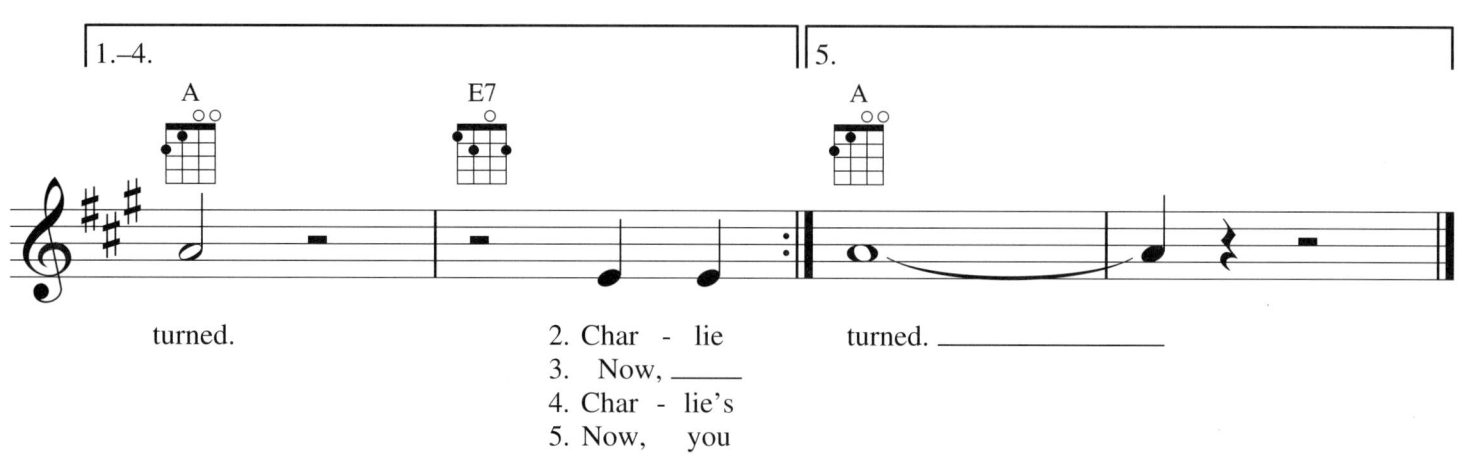

Puff the Magic Dragon

Words and Music by Lenny Lipton and Peter Yarrow

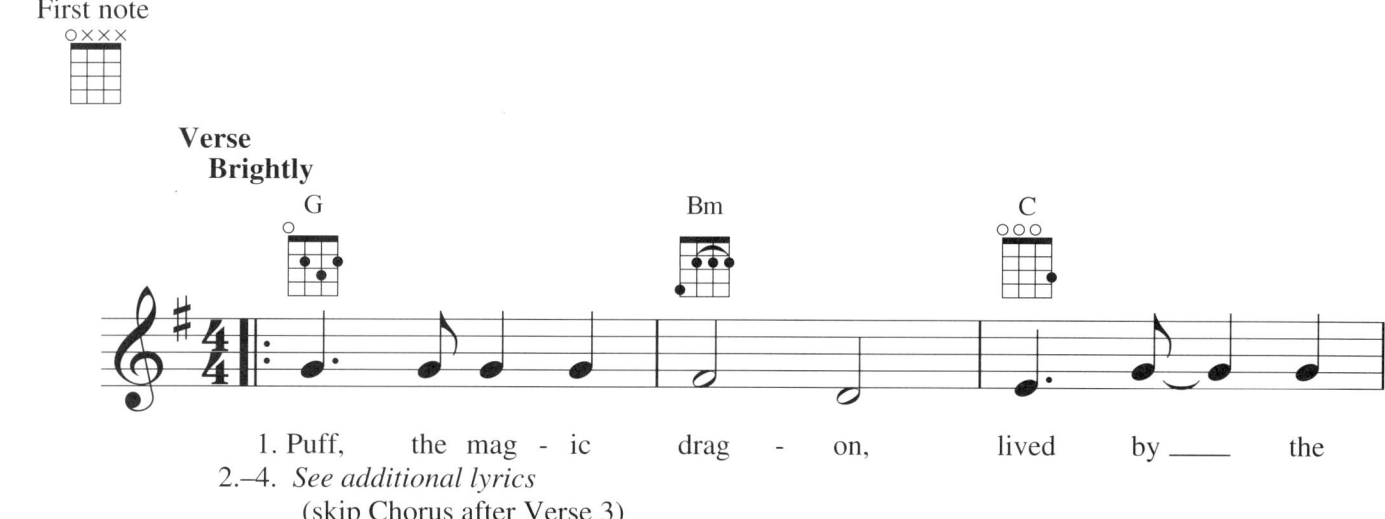

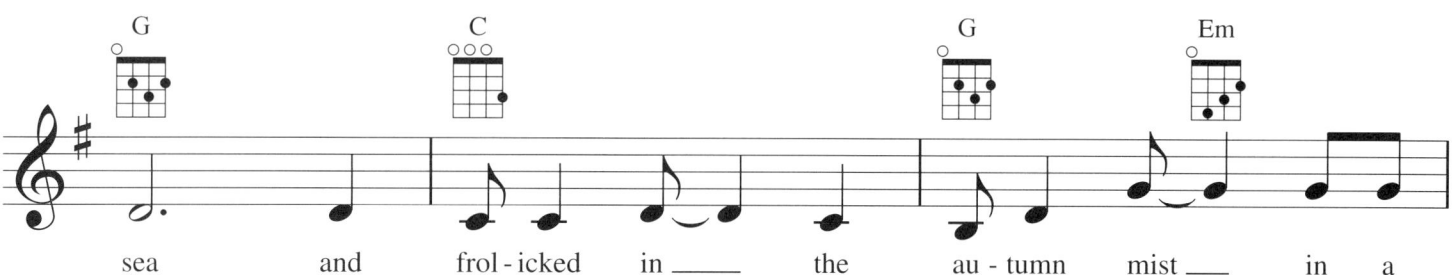

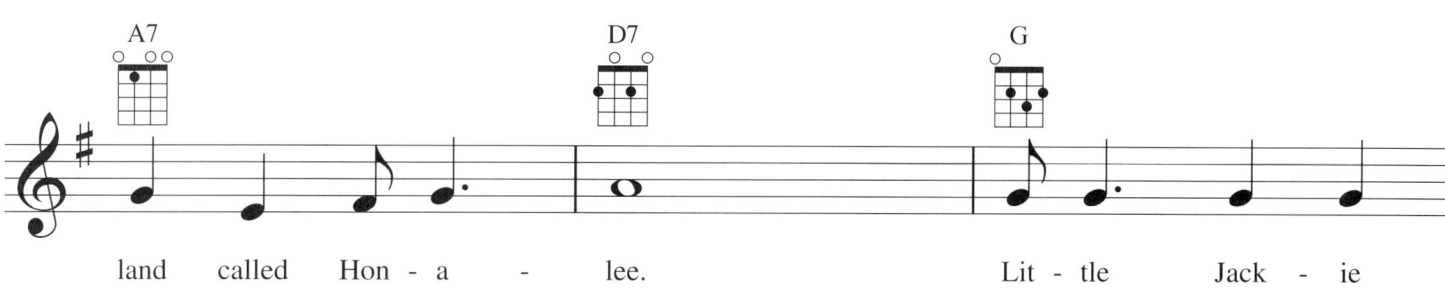

Copyright © 1963; Renewed 1991 Honalee Melodies (ASCAP) and Silver Dawn Music (ASCAP)
Worldwide Rights for Honalee Melodies Administered by BMG Rights Management (US) LLC
Worldwide Rights for Silver Dawn Music Administered by WB Music Corp.
International Copyright Secured   All Rights Reserved

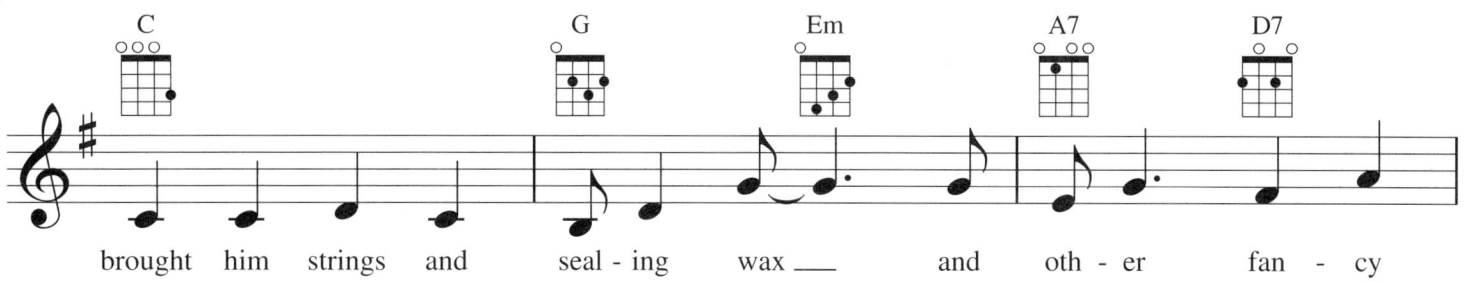

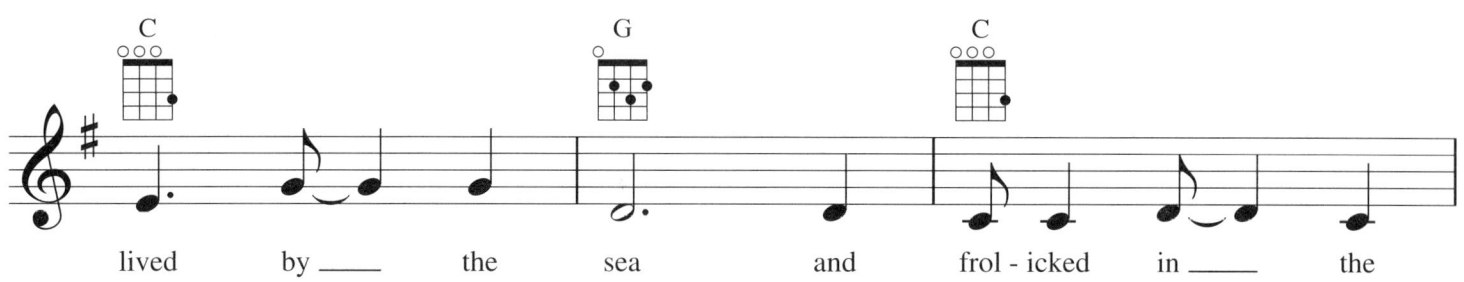
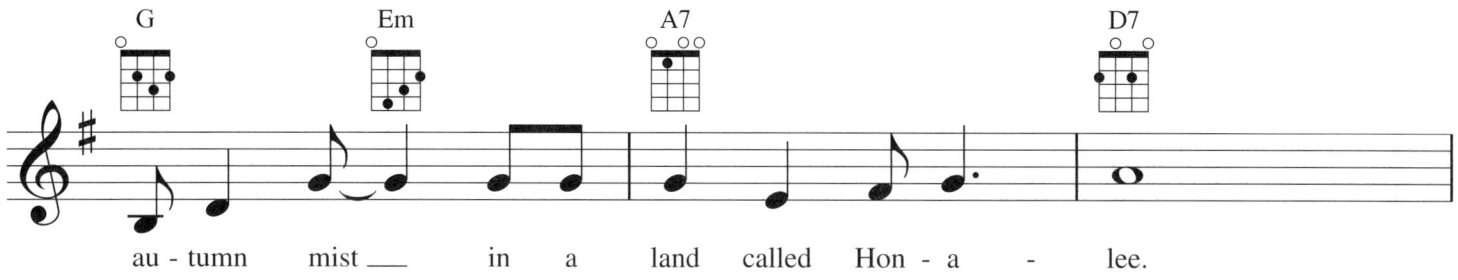

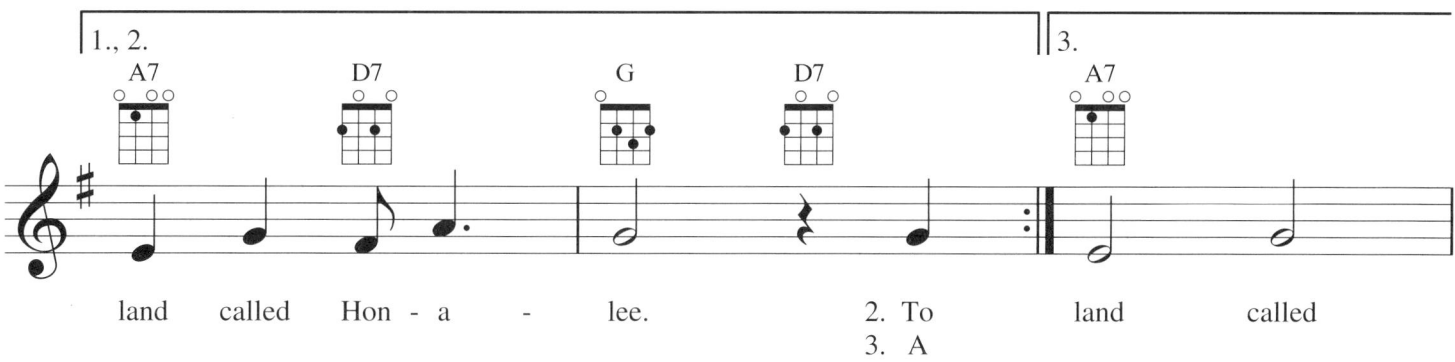
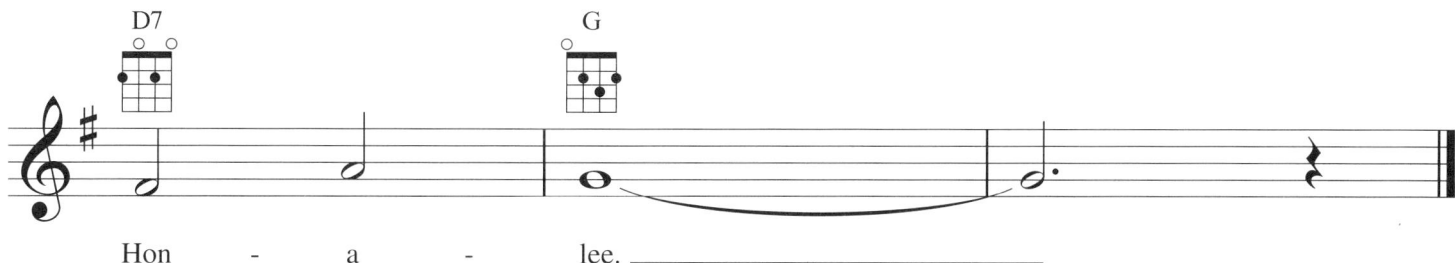

Additional Lyrics

2. Together they would travel on a boat with billowed sail,
   And Jackie kept a lookout perched on Puff's gigantic tail.
   Noble kings and princes would bow whenever they came.
   Pirate ships would lower their flags when Puff roared out his name.

3. A dragon lives forever, but not so little boys.
   Painted wings and giant rings make way for other toys.
   One gray night it happened; Jackie Paper came no more,
   And Puff, that mighty dragon, he ceased his fearless roar. *(To Verse 4)*

4. His head was bent in sorrow, green tears fell like rain.
   Puff no longer went to play along the Cherry Lane.
   Without his lifelong friend, Puff could not be brave.
   So Puff, that mighty dragon, sadly slipped into his cave.

Rock Island Line

Words and Music by Huddie Ledbetter

First note

Fast Blues

𝄋 **Chorus**

'Cause the Rock Is-land line, __ it's a might-y good road, __ 'cause the

Rock Is-land line, __ it's the road __ to ride. __ 'Cause the

Rock Is-land line, __ it's a might-y good road. __ If you

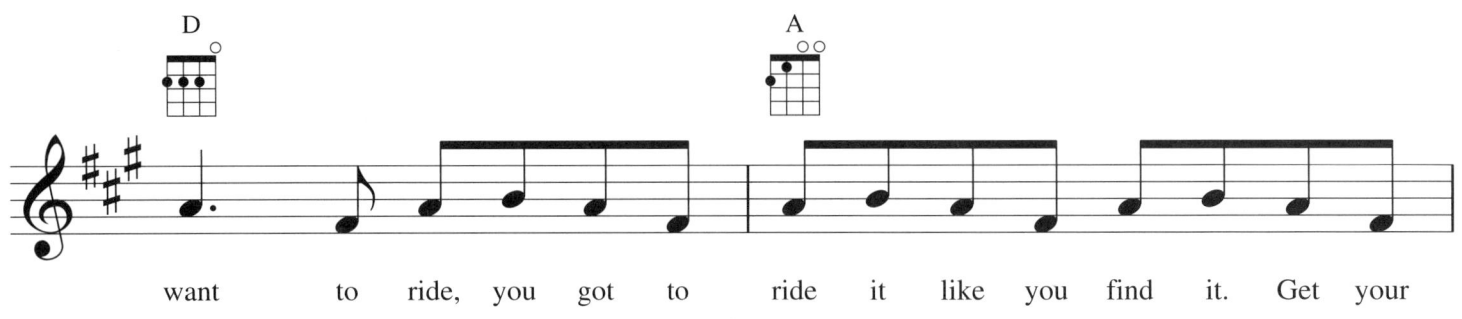
want to ride, you got to ride it like you find it. Get your

© 1959 (Renewed 1987) BEECHWOOD MUSIC CORP.
All Rights Reserved   International Copyright Secured   Used by Permission

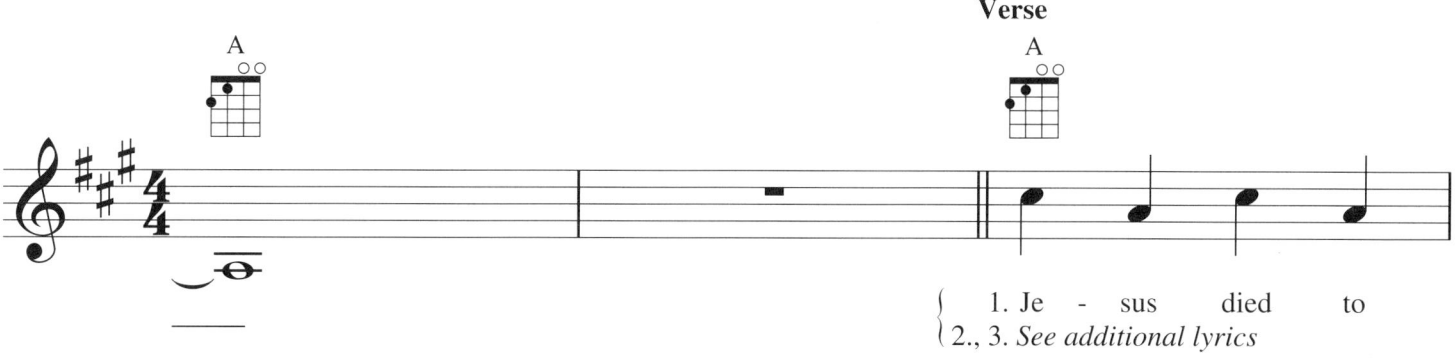

Additional Lyrics

2. A, B, C, W, X, Y, Z,
   The cat's in the cupboard but he don't see me.

3. I may be right and I may be wrong.
   Know you're gonna miss me when I'm gone.

San Francisco Bay Blues

Words and Music by Jesse Fuller

TRO - © Copyright 1958 (Renewed) and 1963 (Renewed) Hollis Music, Inc., New York, NY
International Copyright Secured
All Rights Reserved Including Public Performance For Profit
Used by Permission

Sloop John B.

**Words and Music by Phil F. Sloan,
Steve Barri, Barry McGuire and Bones Howe**

First note
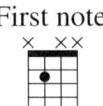

With a Calypso beat

1. We came on the Sloop John B., my grand-fa-ther and me. 'Round Nas-sau town we did roam. Drink-in' all night, had man-y a fight.
(2.) first mate, he got so drunk, he broke o-pen my trunk. Poor sea-sick me on the foam. O-ceans are grand, but give me the land.
(3.) cook went and got the fits, he poured beer on my grits. In-to my soup went his comb. Oh, what a trip, this mis-'ra-ble ship.

I

Copyright © 1965 SONGS OF UNIVERSAL, INC.
Copyright Renewed
All Rights Reserved   Used by Permission

Son-of-a-Preacher Man

Words and Music by John Hurley and Ronnie Wilkins

First note
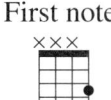

Verse
Lively

1. Jim-my Ray was a preach-er's son when his
2. *See additional lyrics*

dad-dy would vis-it he'd come ___ a-long. When they gath-ered 'round the

par-lor talk-in', cous-in Jim-my would talk me walk-in'

out thru the back yard we'd go walk-in', and then he'd look in-

Copyright © 1968 Sony/ATV Music Publishing LLC
Copyright Renewed
All Rights Administered by Sony/ATV Music Publishing LLC, 8 Music Square West, Nashville, TN 37203
International Copyright Secured   All Rights Reserved

to my eyes. ____ Lord knows, to my sur - prise, the

Chorus

on - ly one who could ev - er reach me was the son - of - a -

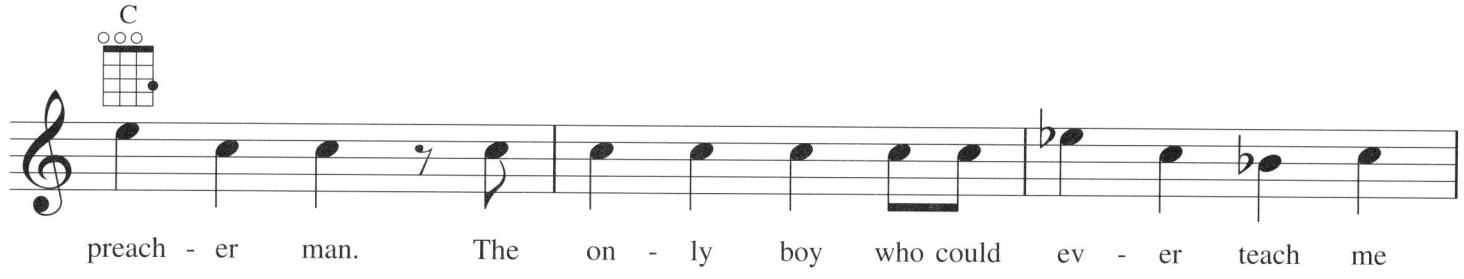
preach - er man. The on - ly boy who could ev - er teach me

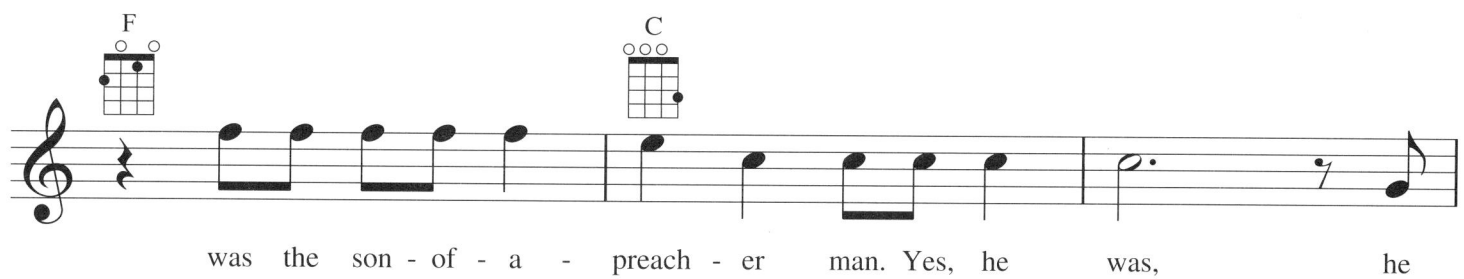
was the son - of - a - preach - er man. Yes, he was, he

1.
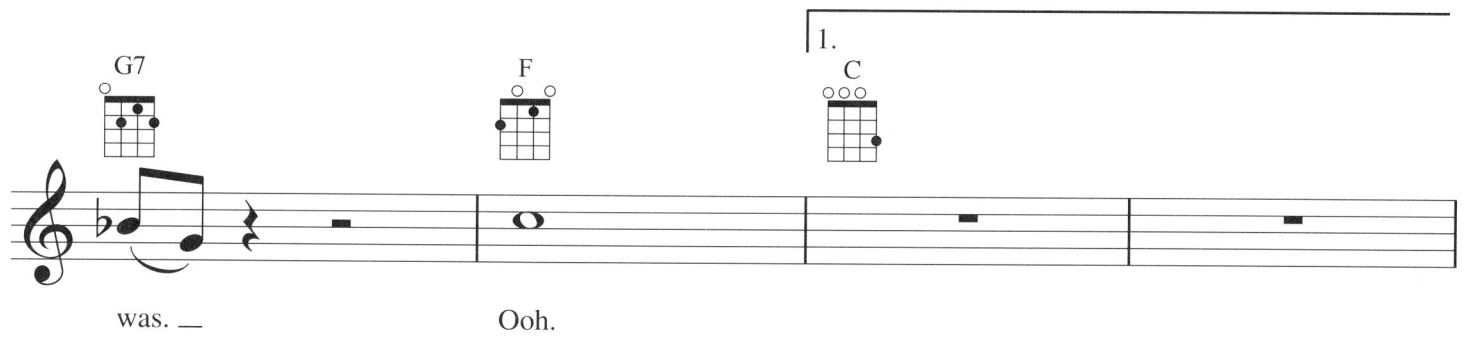
was. ____ Ooh.

2.
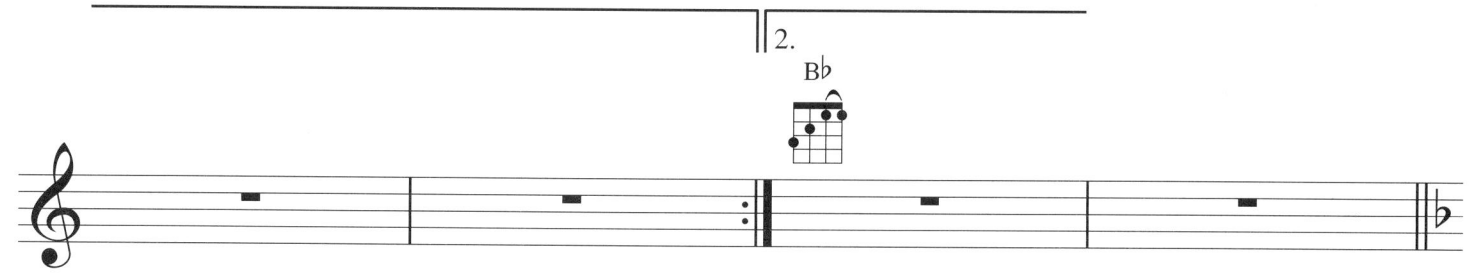

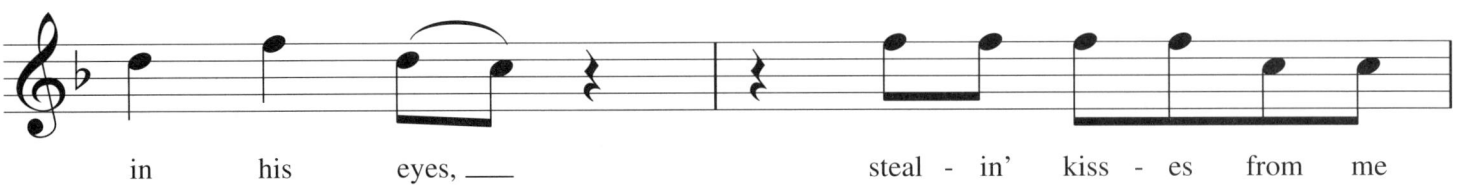
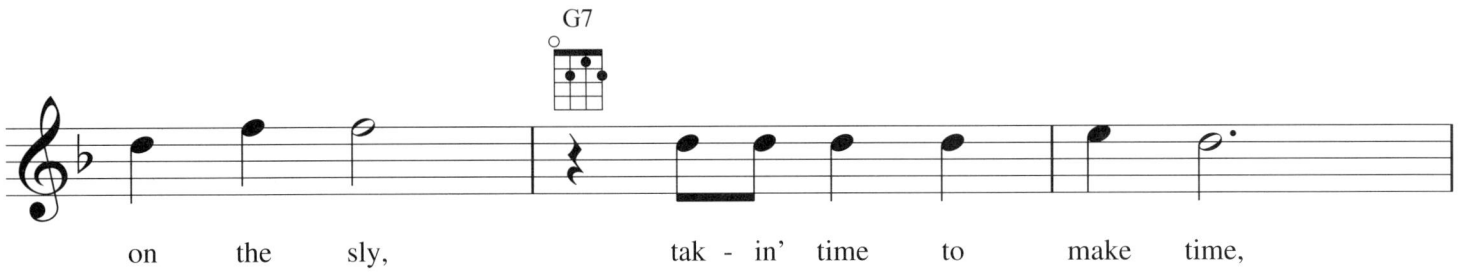
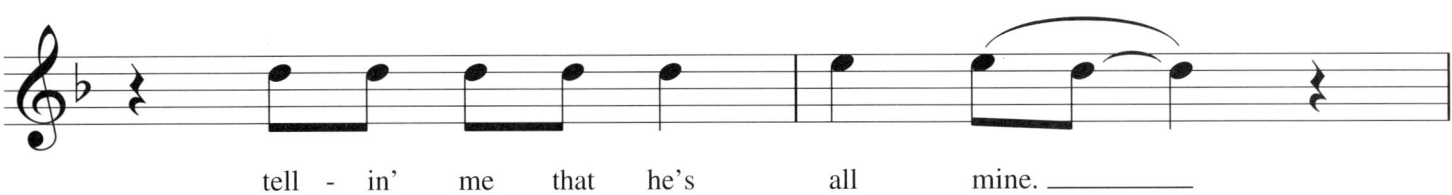
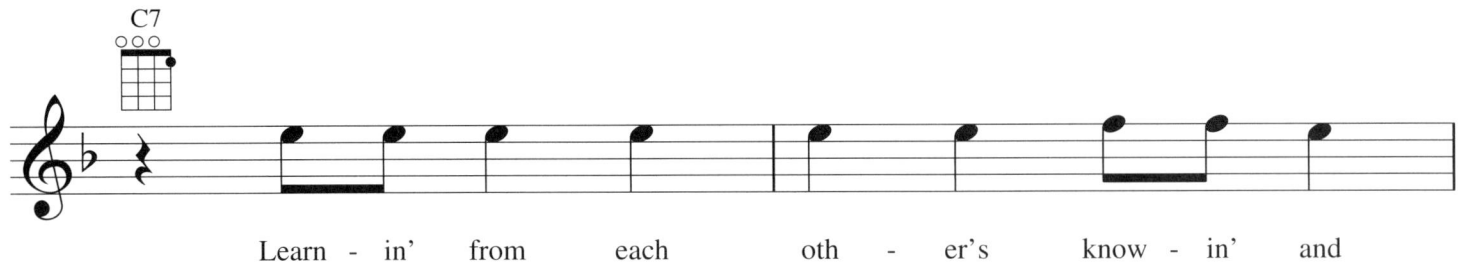
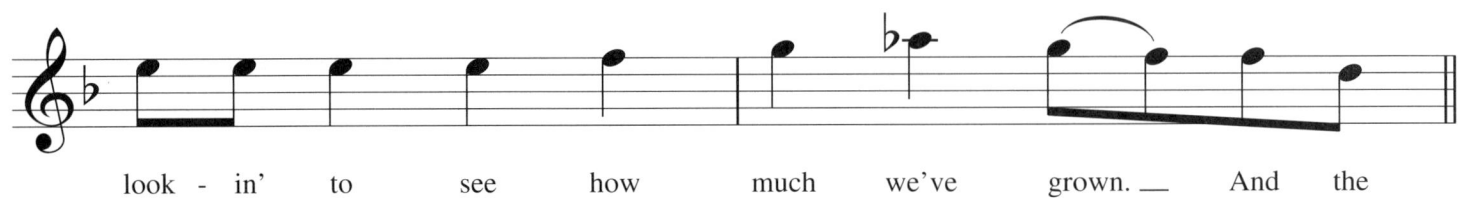

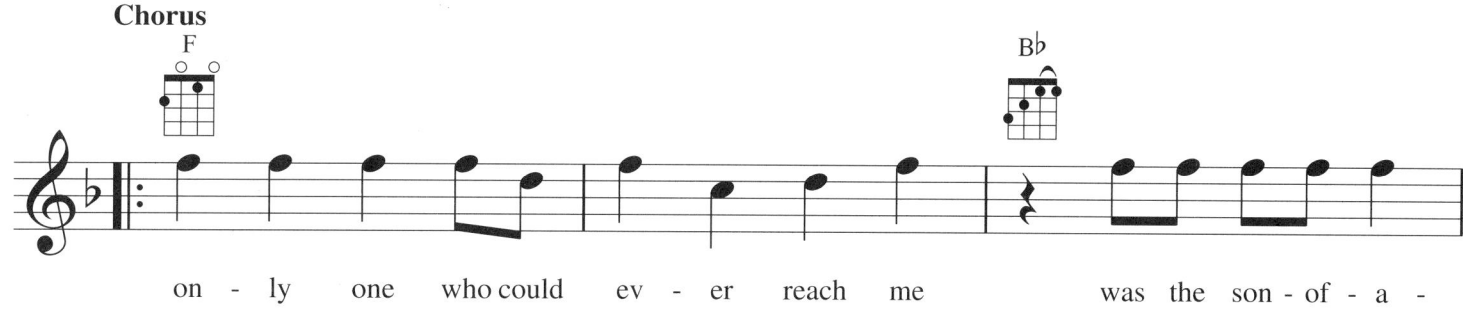
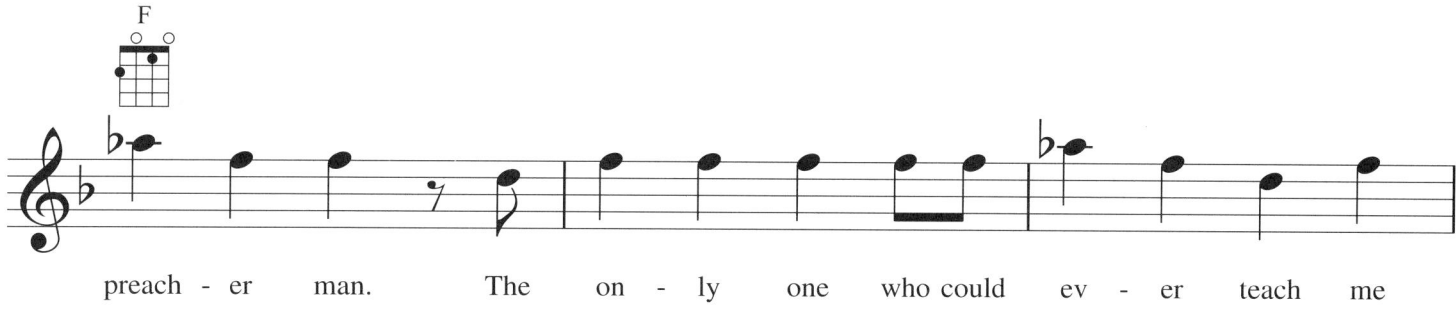
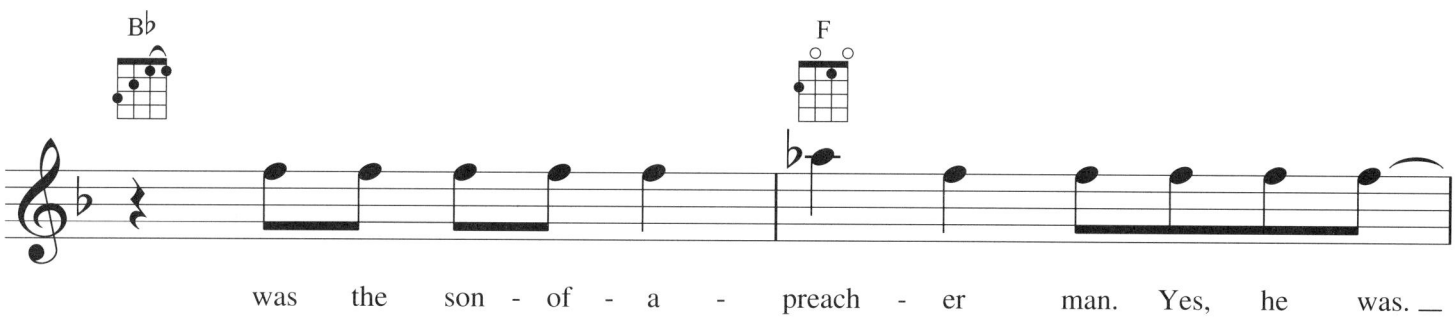

Additional Lyrics

2. Being good isn't always easy no matter how I try.
   When he started sweet talkin' to me, he'd come and tell me ev'rything is alright;
   Kiss and tell me ev'rything is alright, and "Can I sneak away again tonight?"
   Lord knows, to my surprise,...

Tom Dooley

Words and Music Collected, Adapted and Arranged by Frank Warner, John A. Lomax and Alan Lomax
From the singing of Frank Proffitt

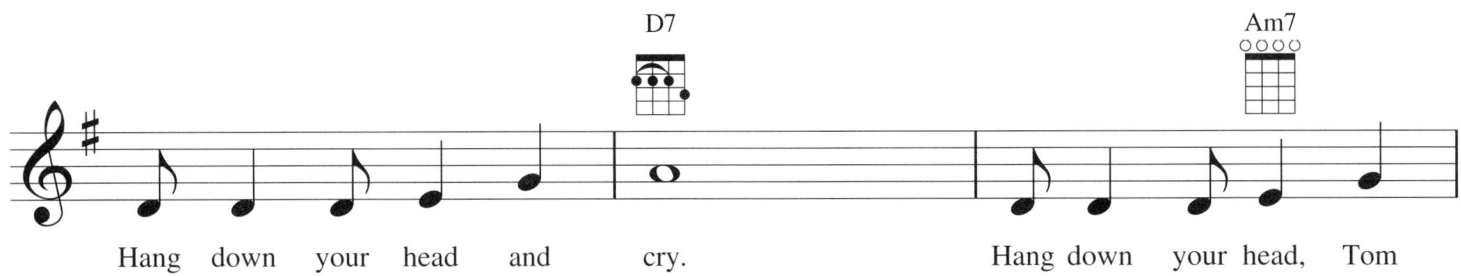
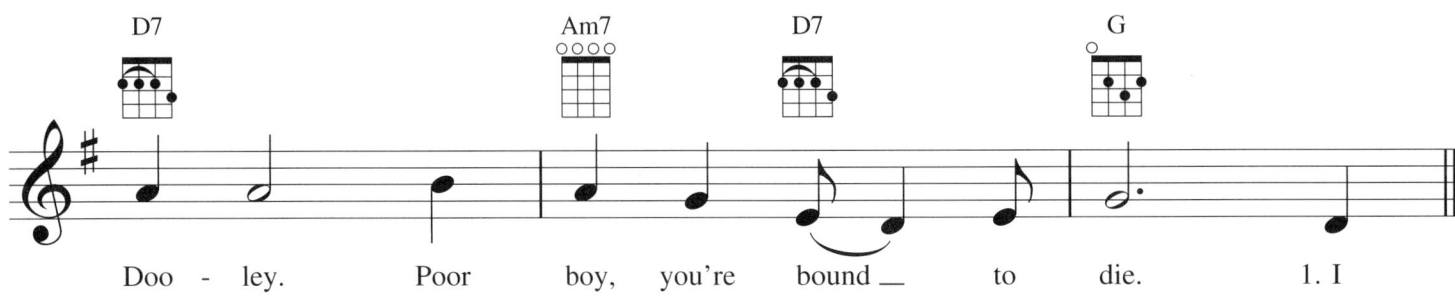
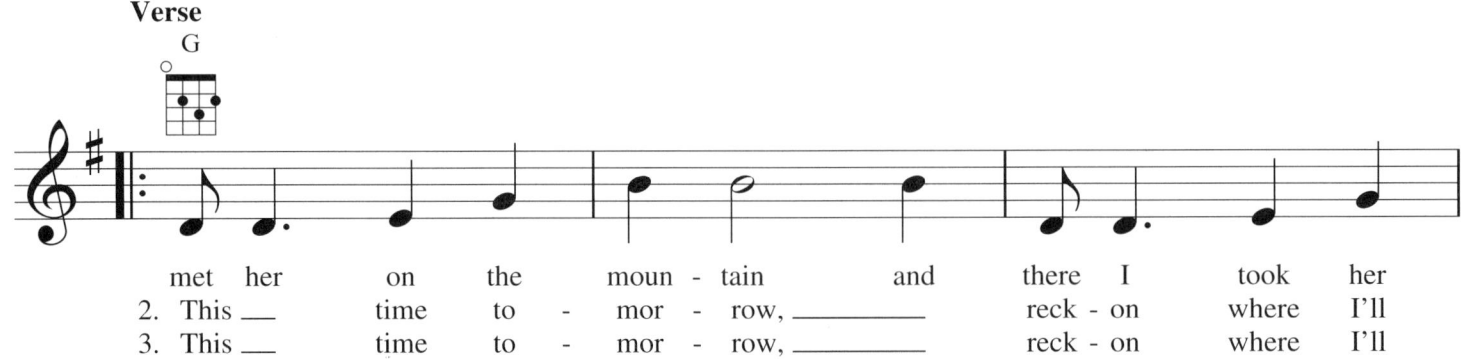

TRO - © Copyright 1947 (Renewed) and 1958 (Renewed) Ludlow Music, Inc., New York, NY
International Copyright Secured
All Rights Reserved Including Public Performance For Profit
Used by Permission

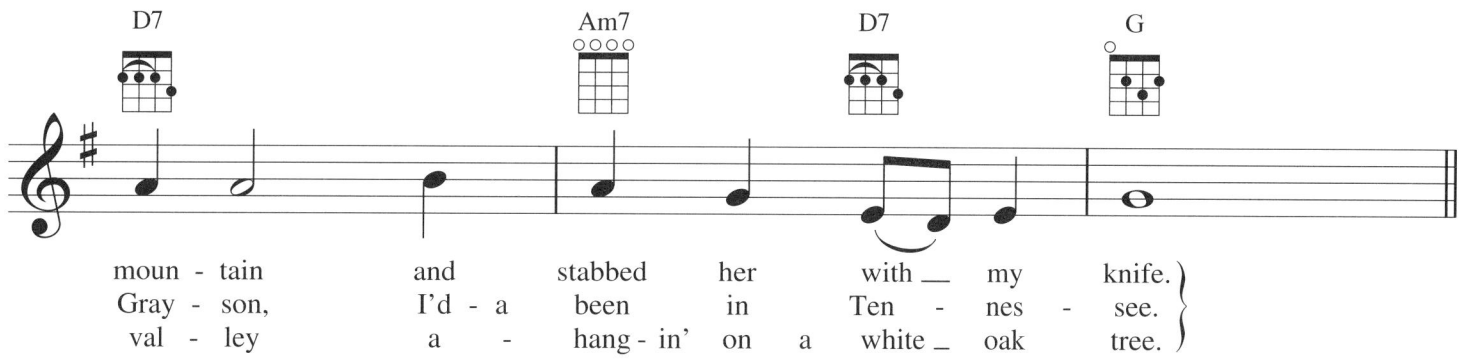

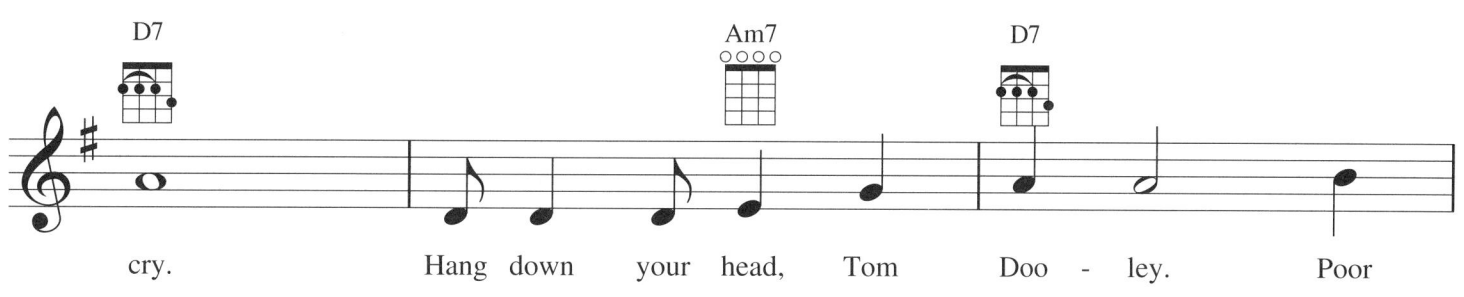
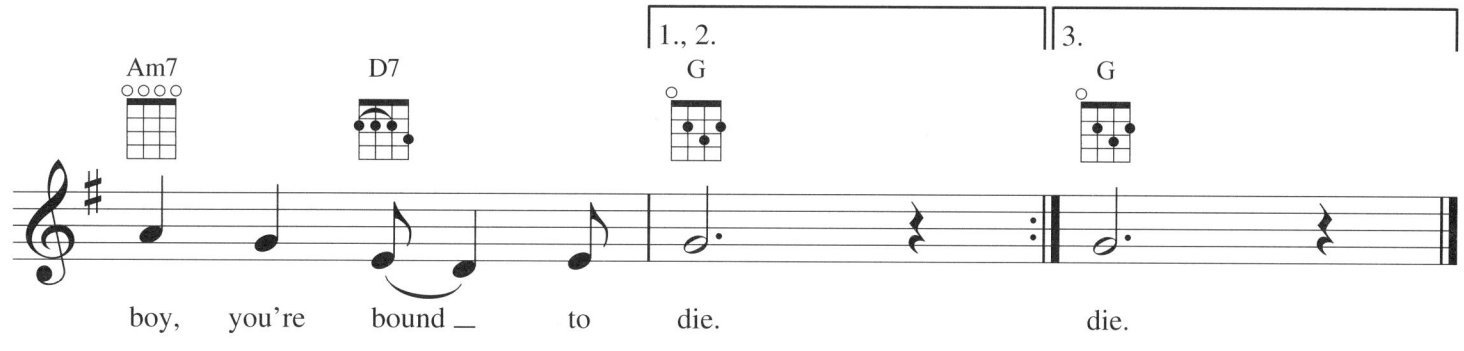

Scotch and Soda

Words and Music by Dave Guard

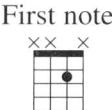
First note

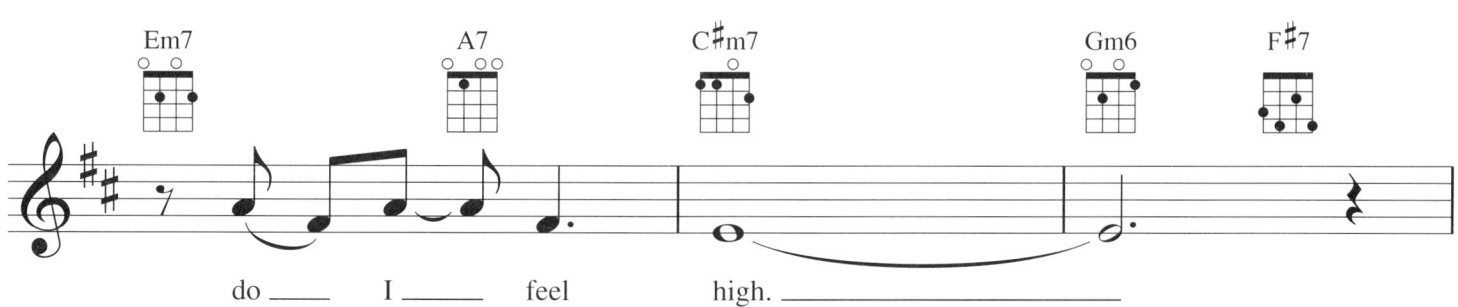

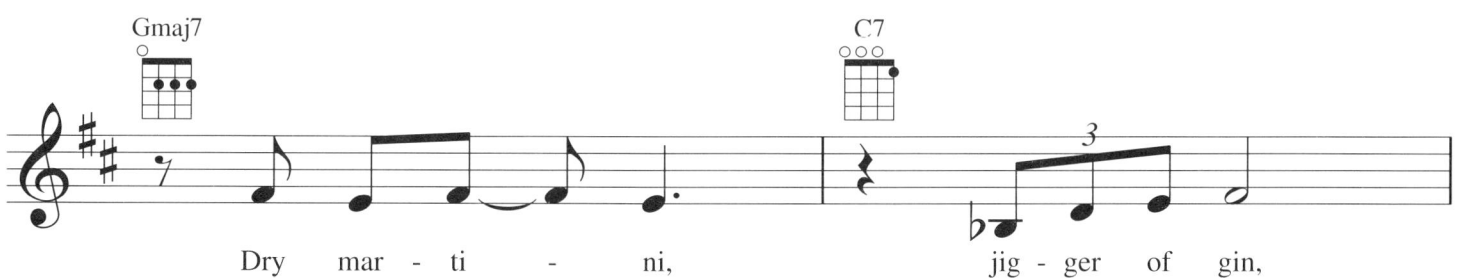

© 1959, 1961 (Renewed 1987, 1989) BEECHWOOD MUSIC CORP.
All Rights Reserved   International Copyright Secured   Used by Permission

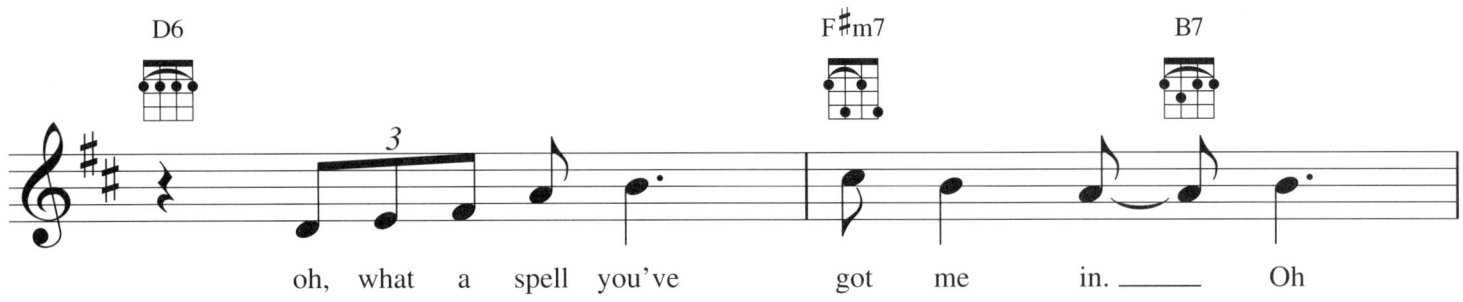
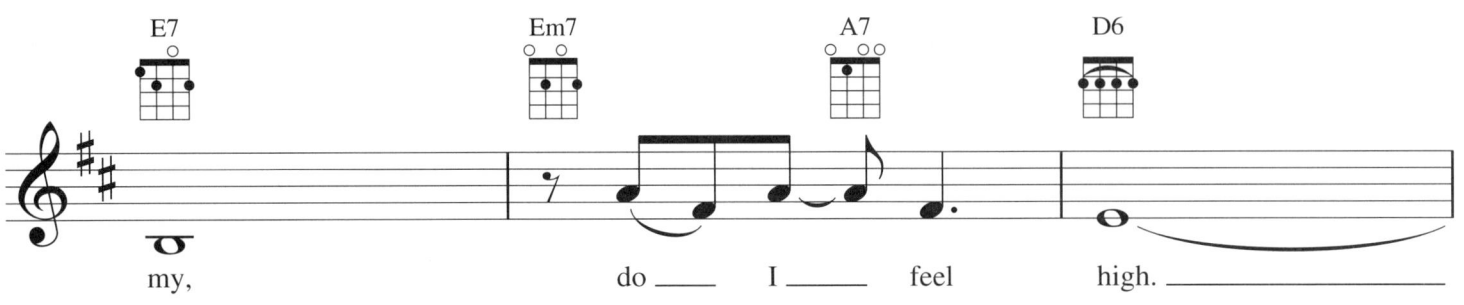
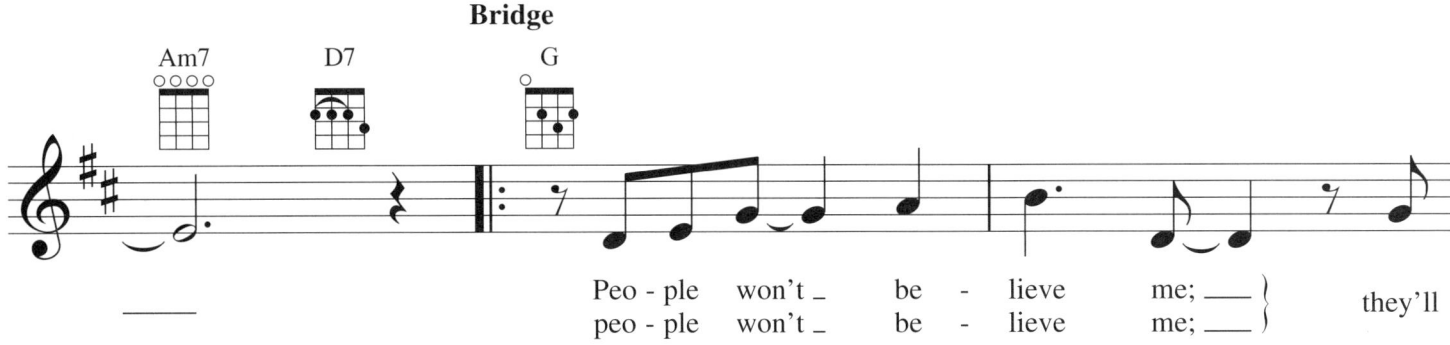
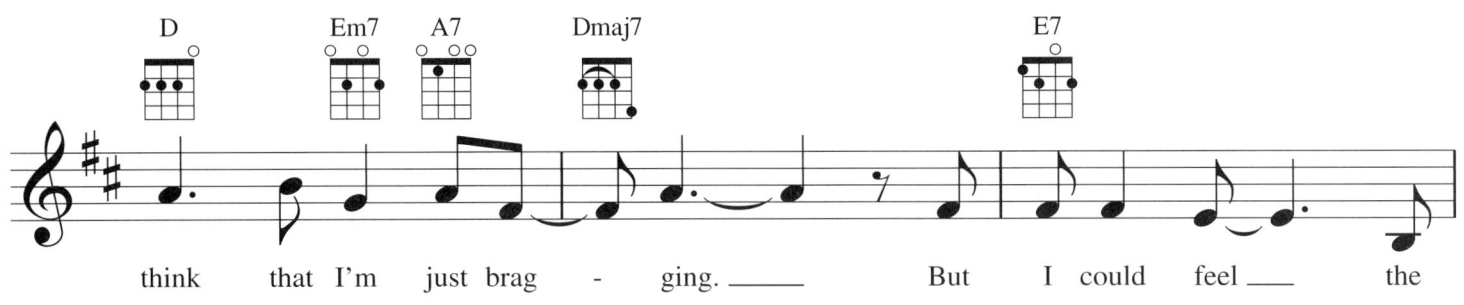
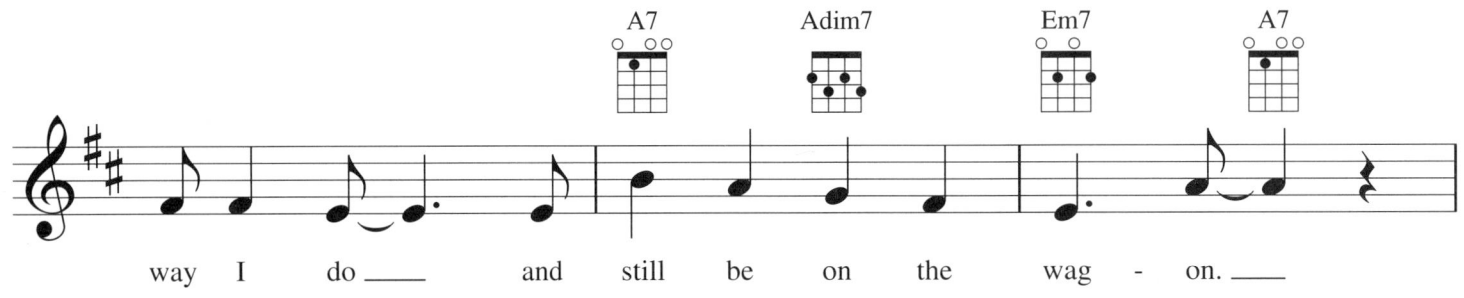

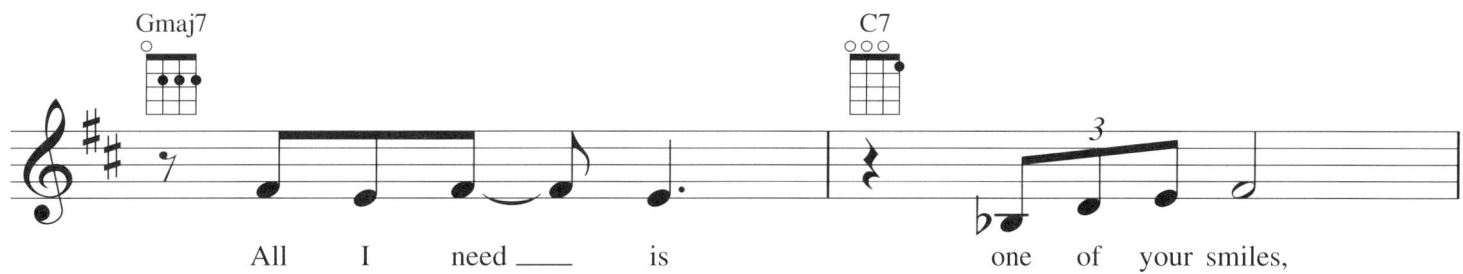

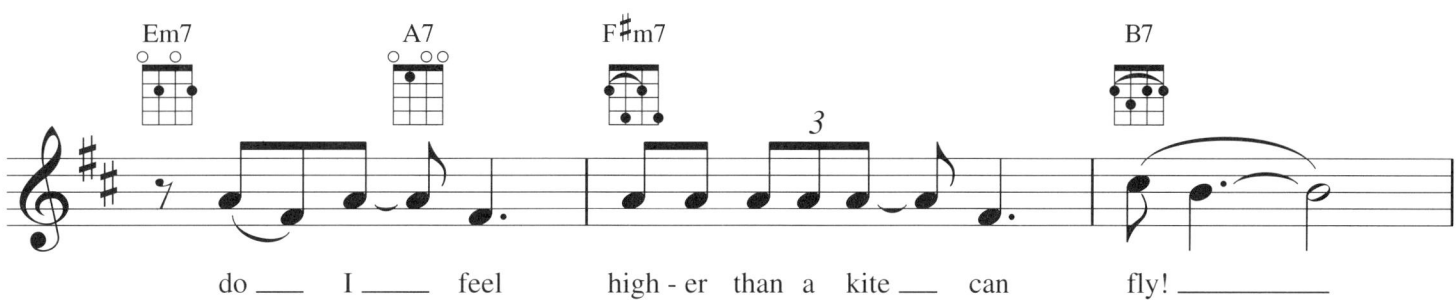
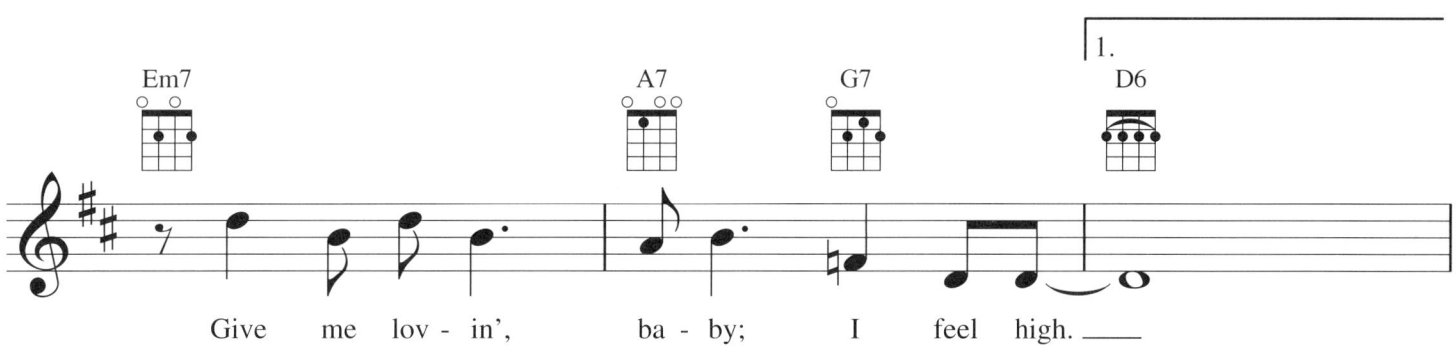
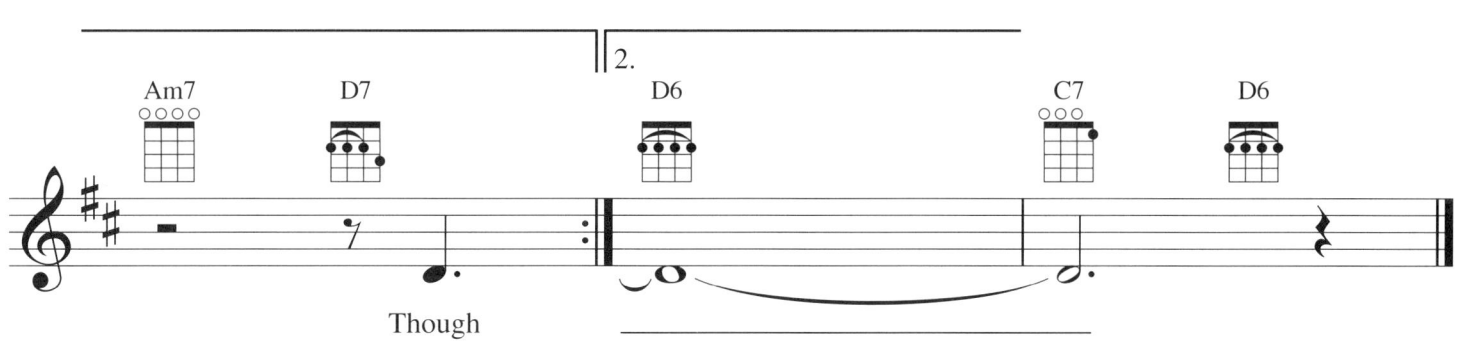

The Unicorn
Words and Music by Shel Silverstein

First note

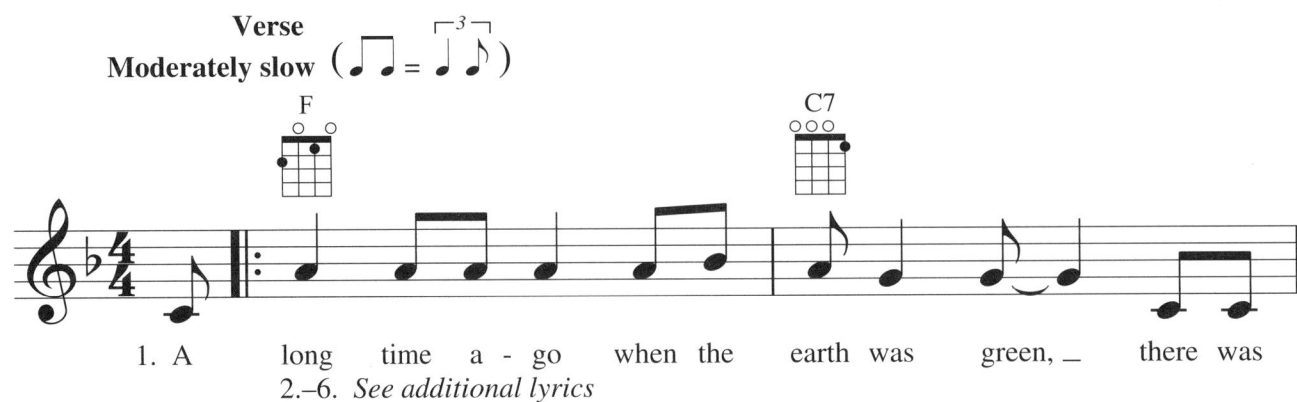

1. A long time a-go when the earth was green, there was
2.–6. See additional lyrics

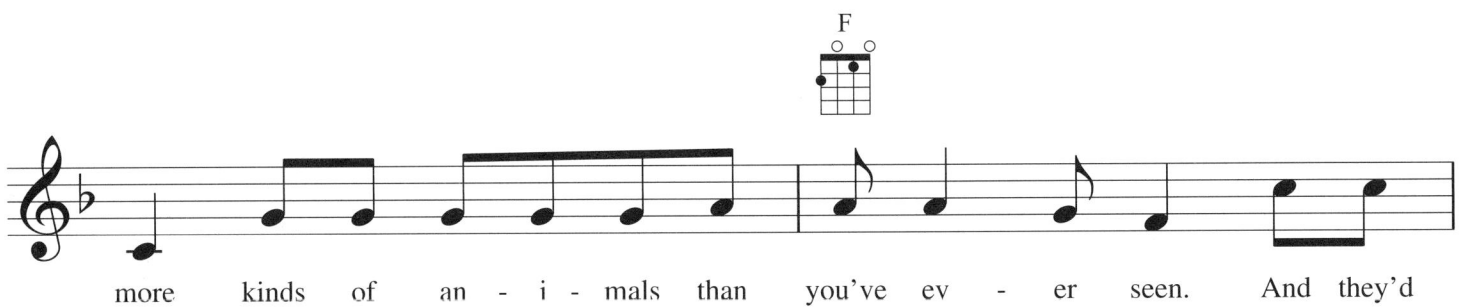

more kinds of an-i-mals than you've ev-er seen. And they'd

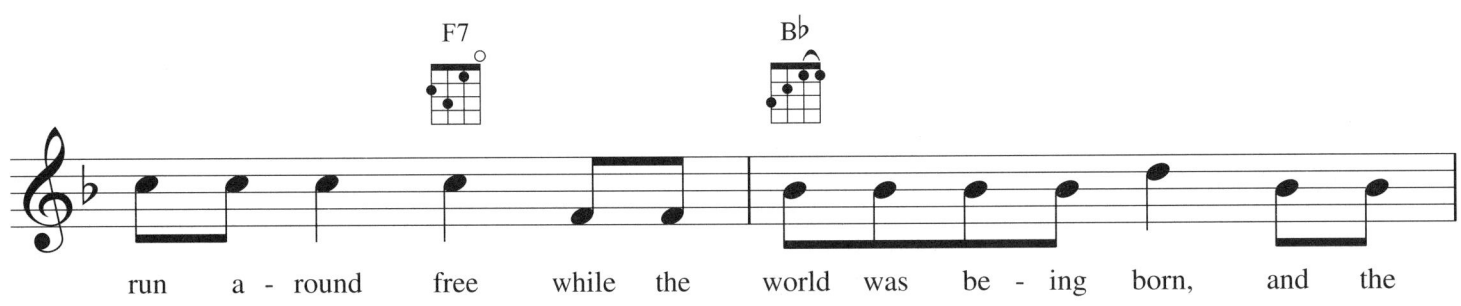

run a-round free while the world was be-ing born, and the

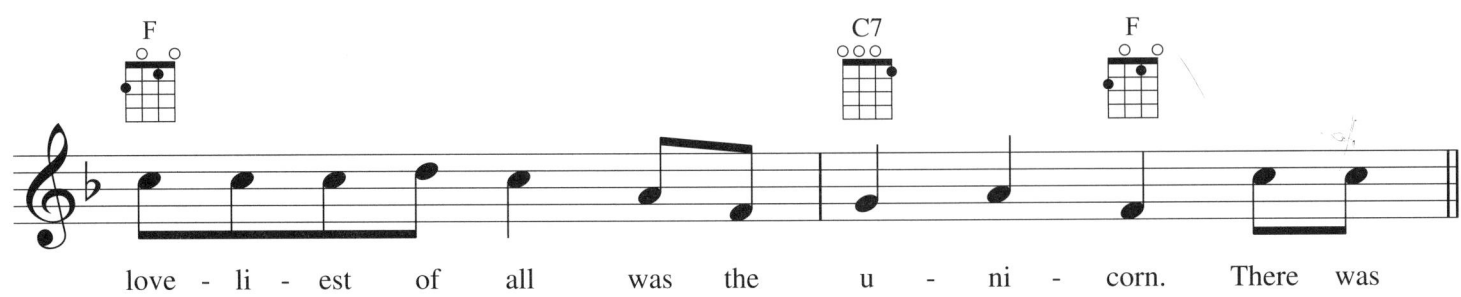

love-li-est of all was the u-ni-corn. There was

TRO - © Copyright 1962 (Renewed) and 1968 (Renewed) Hollis Music, Inc., New York, NY
International Copyright Secured
All Rights Reserved Including Public Performance For Profit
Used by Permission

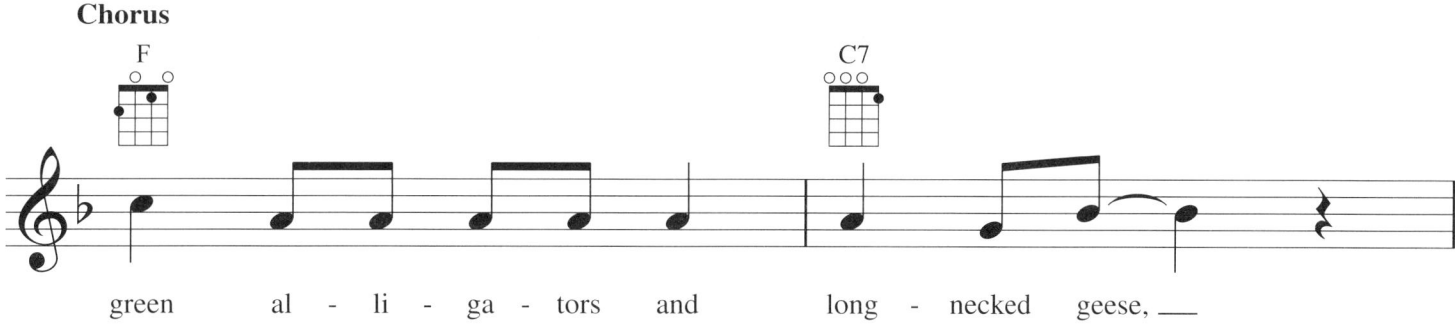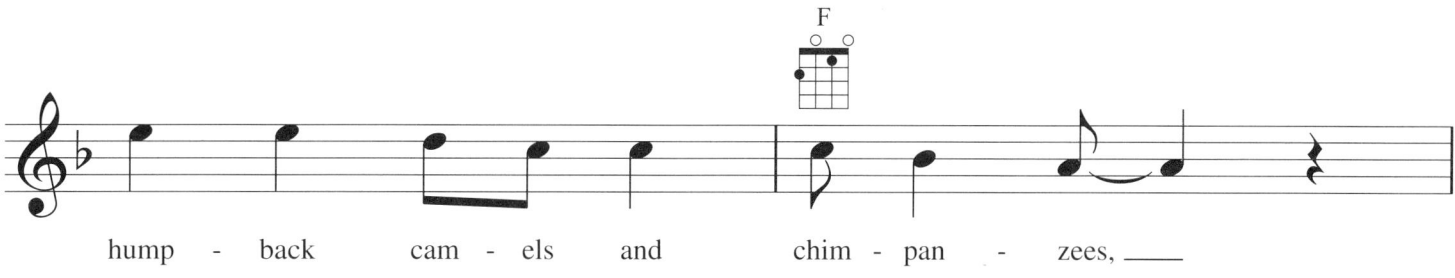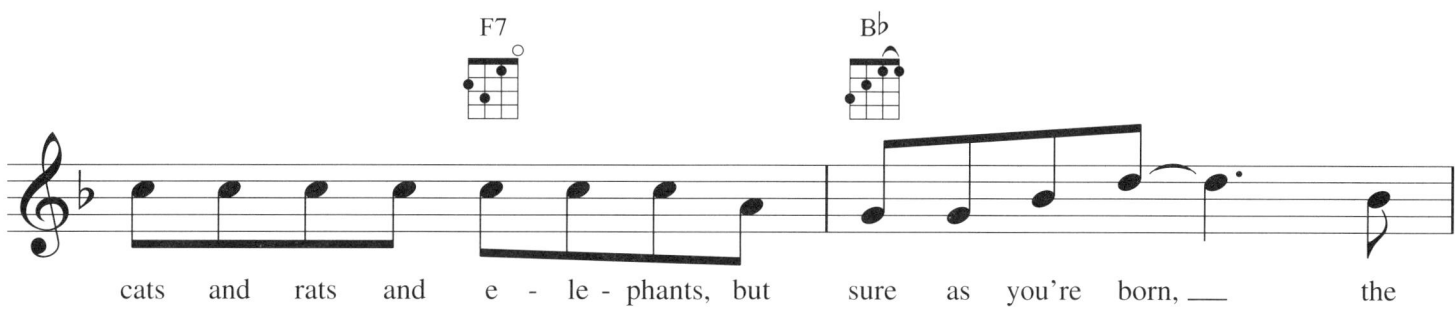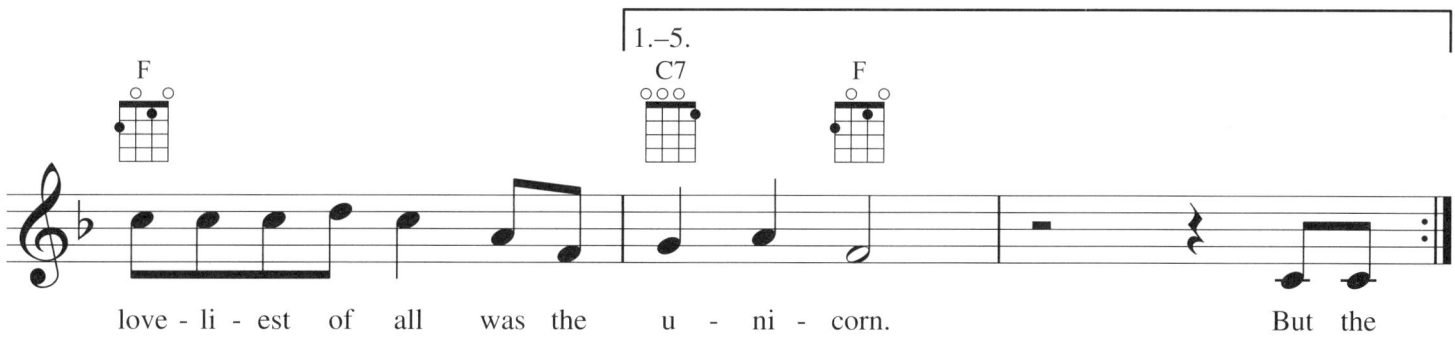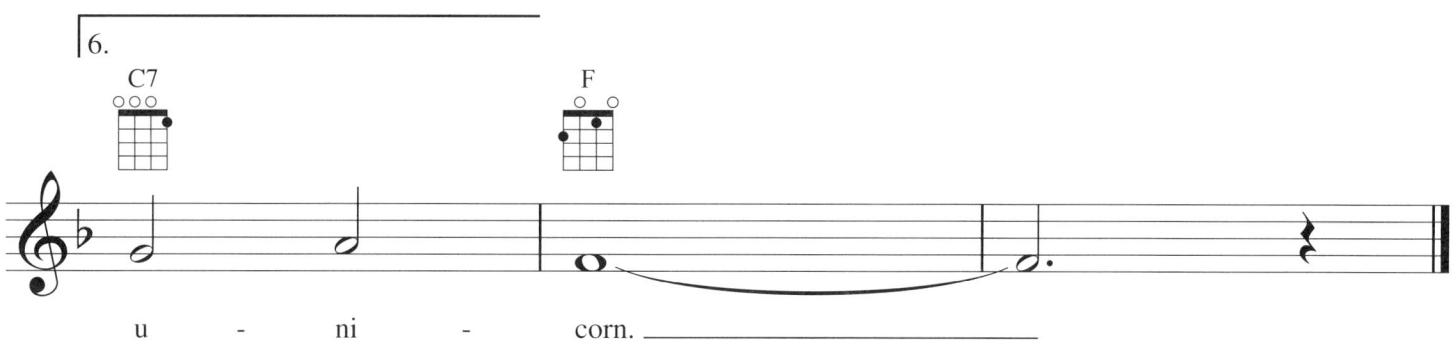

Additional Lyrics

2. But the Lord seen some sinnin' and it caused him pain.
   He says, "Stand back, I'm gonna make it rain.
   So, hey, Brother Noah, I'll tell you what to do,
   Go and build me a floating zoo."
Chorus: "Two alligators and a couple of geese,
   Two hump-back camels and two chimpanzees,
   Two cats, two rats, two elephants, but sure as you're born,
   Noah, don't you forget my unicorns."

3. Now Noah was there and he answered the callin'
   And he finished up the ark as the rain started fallin'.
   Then he marched in the animals two by two,
   And he sung out as they went through:
Chorus: "Hey, Lord, I got you two alligators and a couple of geese,
   Two hump-back camels and two chimpanzees,
   Two cats, two rats, two elephants, but sure as you're born,
   Lord, I don't see your unicorns."

4. Well, Noah looked out through the drivin' rain,
   But the unicorns was hidin' — playin' silly games.
   They were kickin' and a-spashin' while the rain was pourin',
   Oh, them foolish unicorns.
Chorus: "Hey, Lord, I got you two alligators and a couple of geese,
   Two hump-back camels and two chimpanzees,
   Two cats, two rats, two elephants, but sure as you're born,
   Lord, I don't see your unicorns."

5. Then the ducks started duckin' and the snakes started snakin',
   And the elephants started elephantin' and the boat started shakin',
   The mice started squeakin' and the lions started roarin',
   And everyone's aboard but them unicorns.
Chorus: I mean the two alligators and a couple of geese,
   The hump-back camels and the chimpanzees,
   Noah cried, "Close the door 'cause the rain is pourin',
   And we just can't wait for them unicorns."

6. And then the ark started movin' and it drifted with the tide
   And the unicorns looked up from the rock and cried,
   And the water came up and sort of floated them away.
   That's why you've never seen a unicorn to this day.
Chorus: You'll see a lot of alligators and a whole mess of geese,
   You'll see hump-back camels and chimpanzees,
   You'll see cats and rats and elephants, but sure as you're born,
   You're never gonna see no unicorn.

We'll Sing in the Sunshine

Words and Music by Gale Garnett

First note

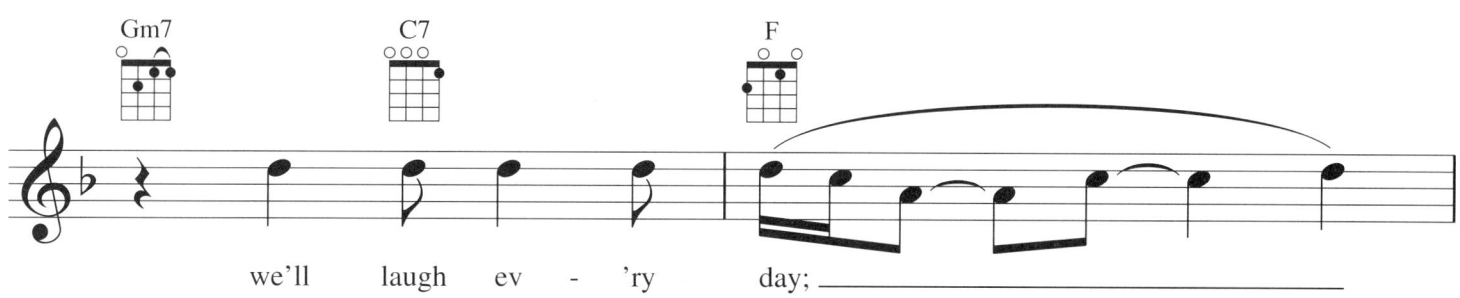

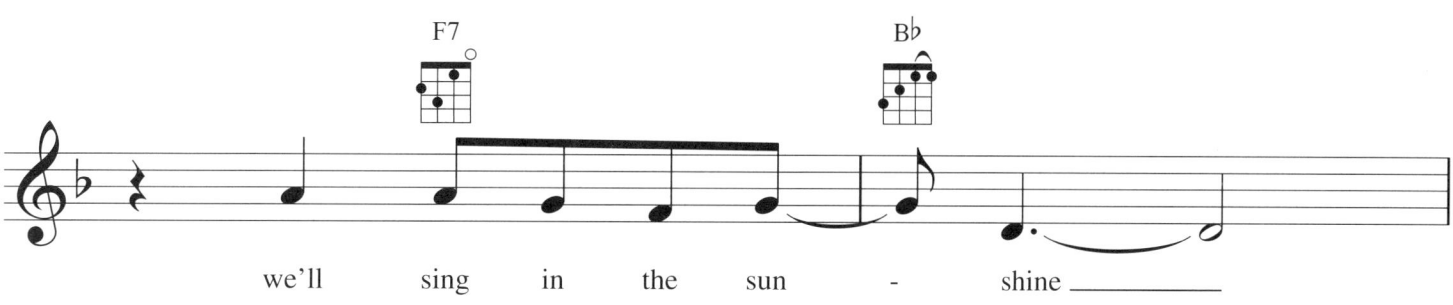

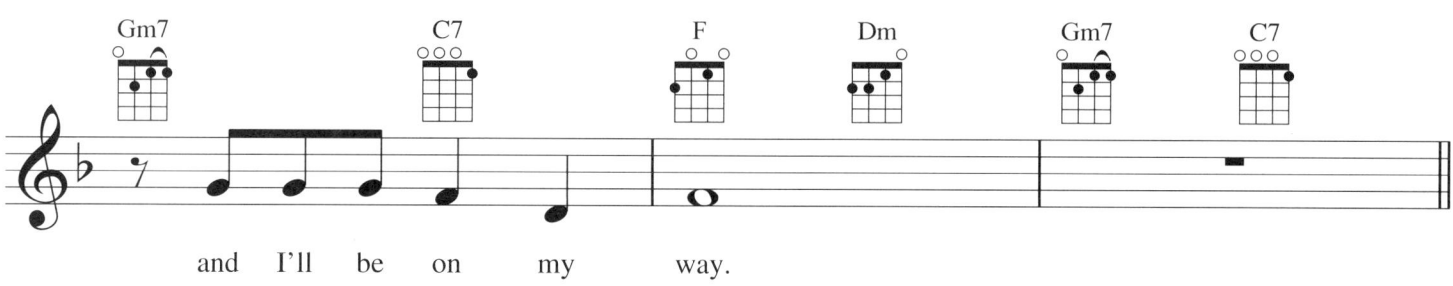

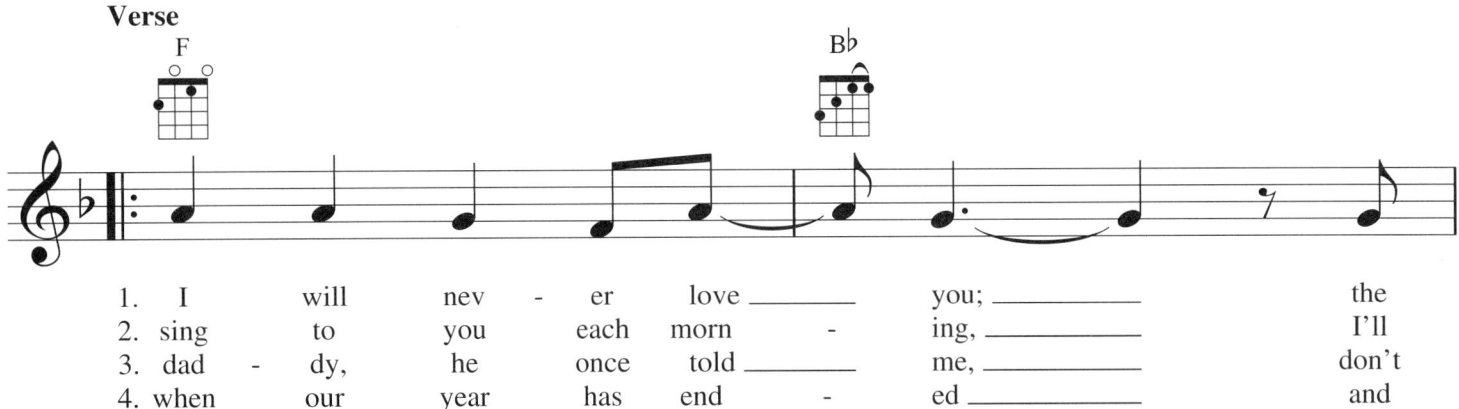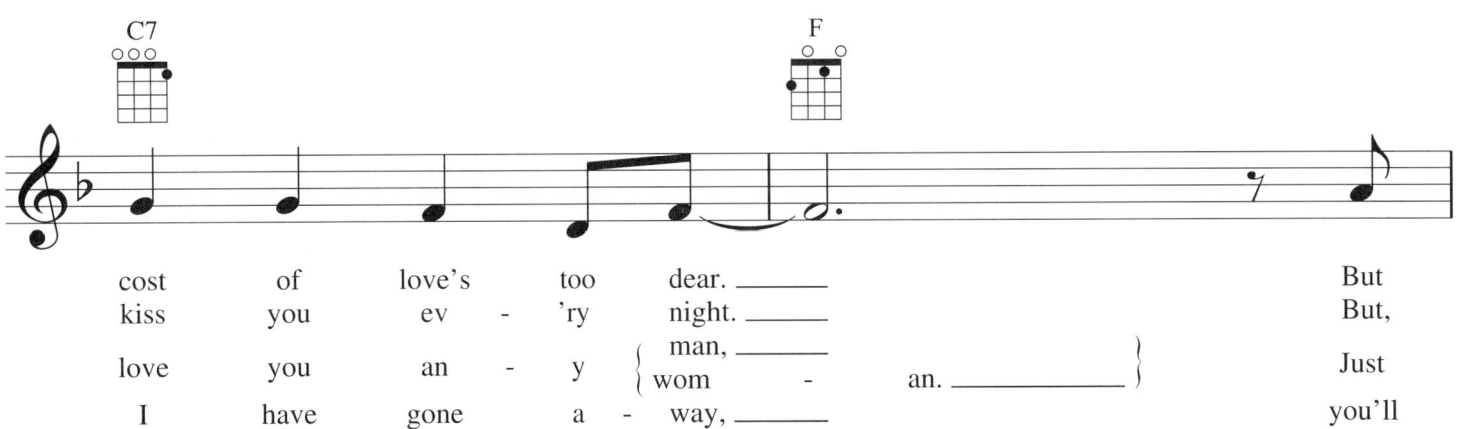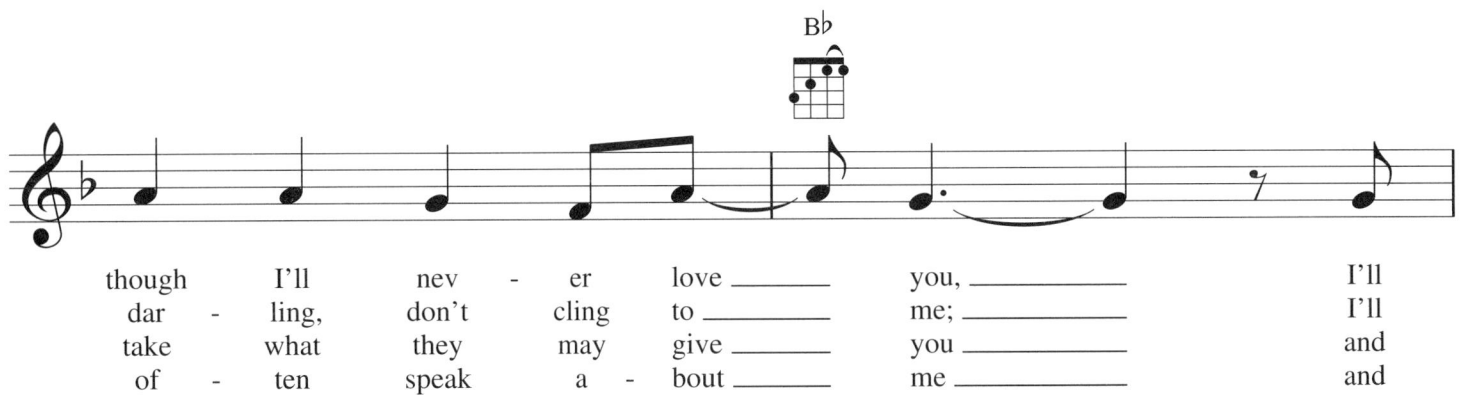

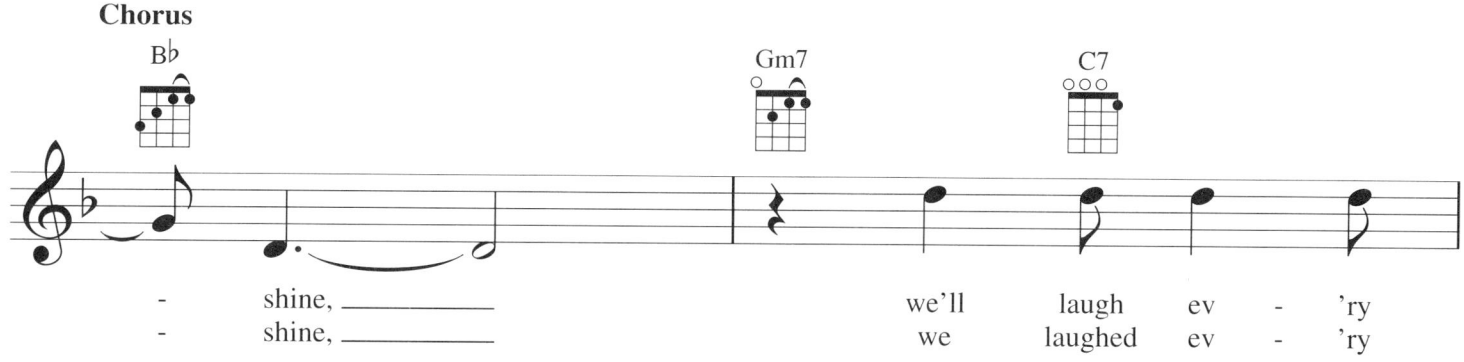
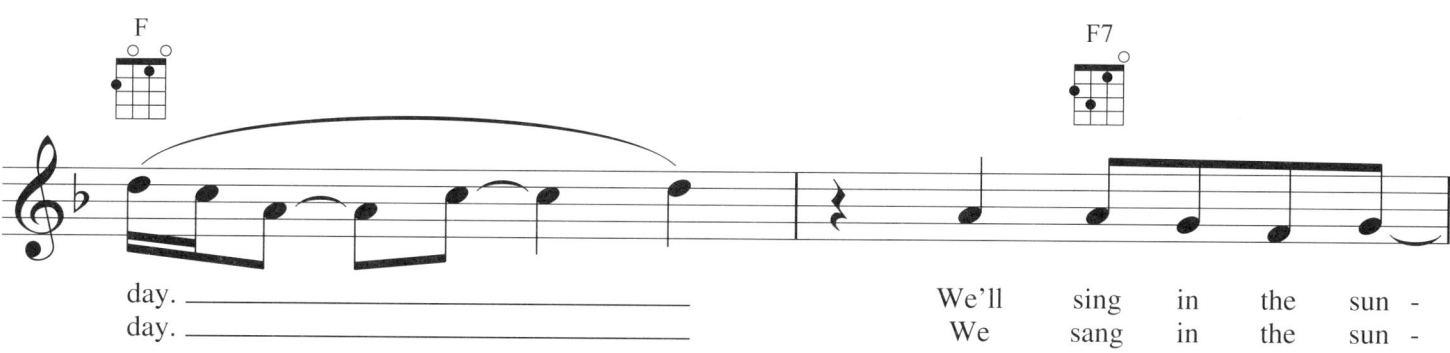
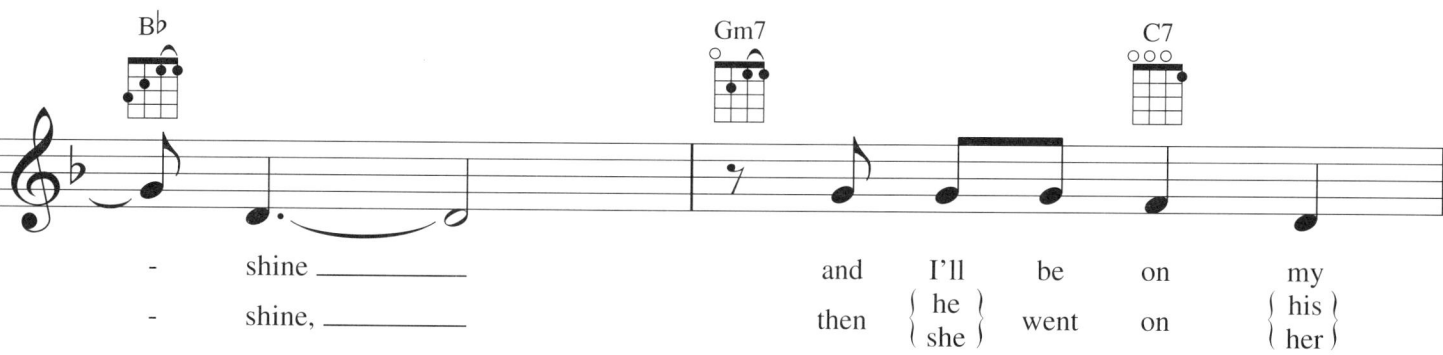
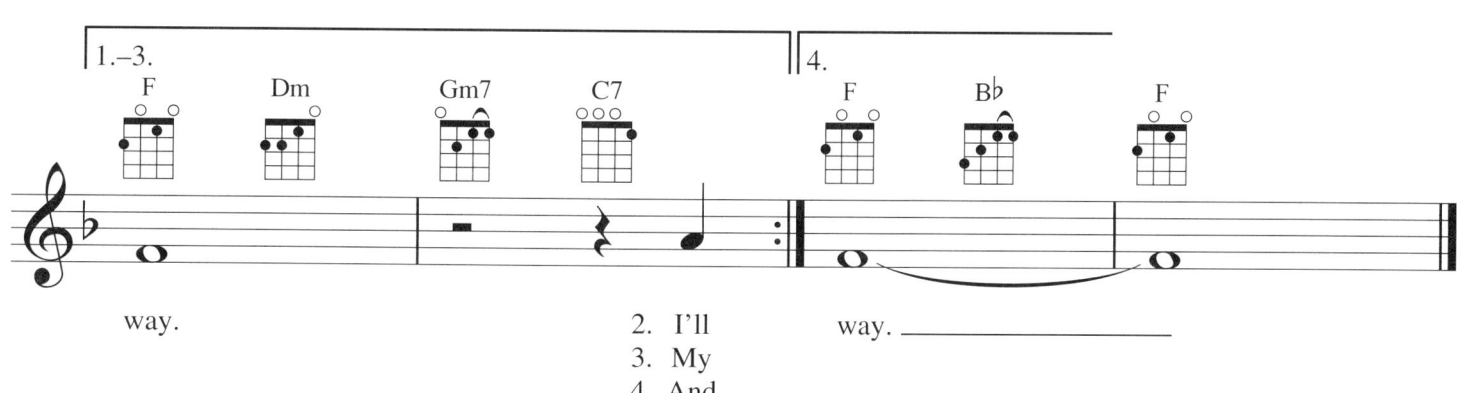

69

Walk Right In

Words and Music by Gus Cannon and H. Woods

First note

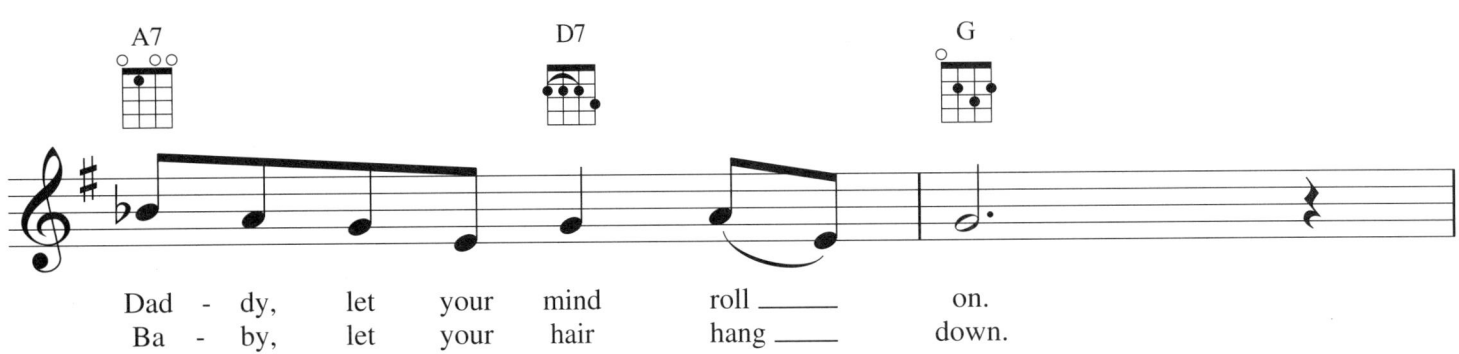

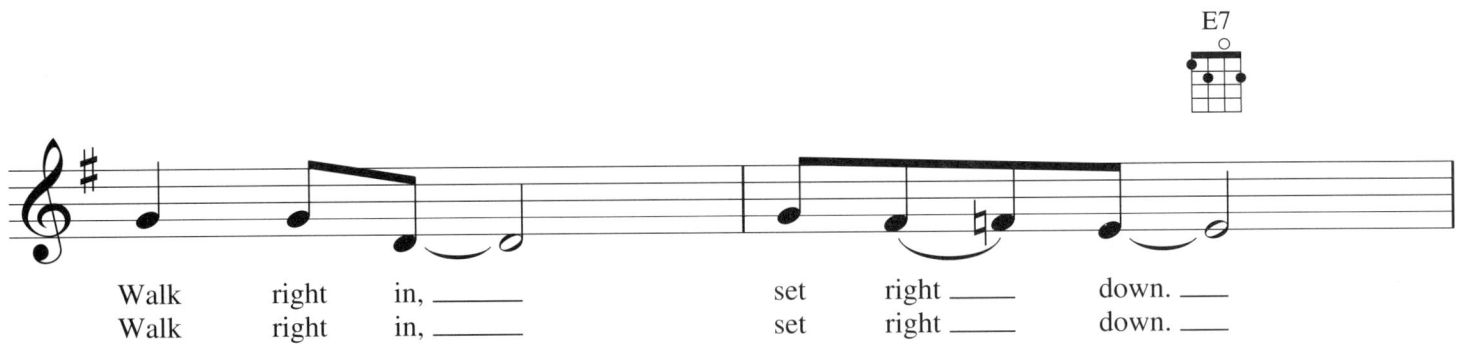

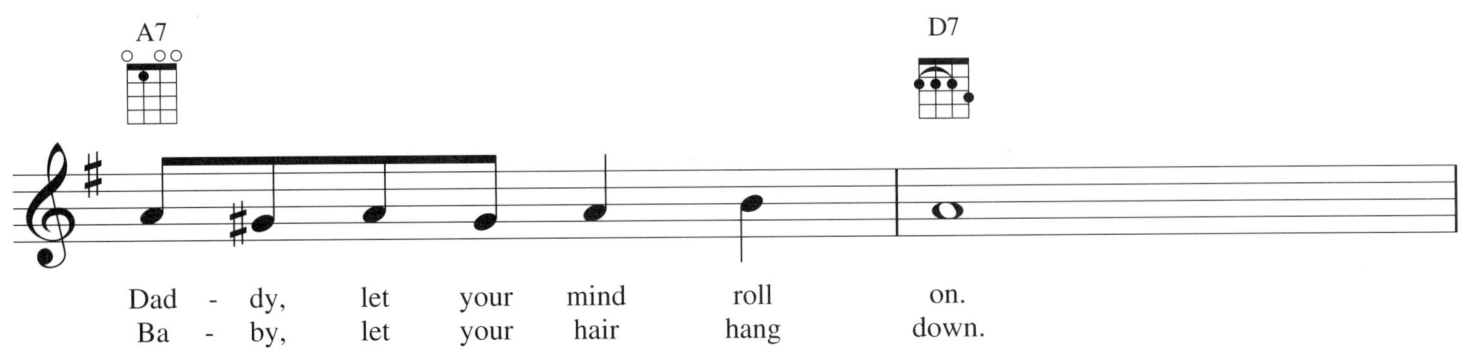

Copyright © 1930 by Peer International Corporation
Copyright Renewed
International Copyright Secured All Rights Reserved

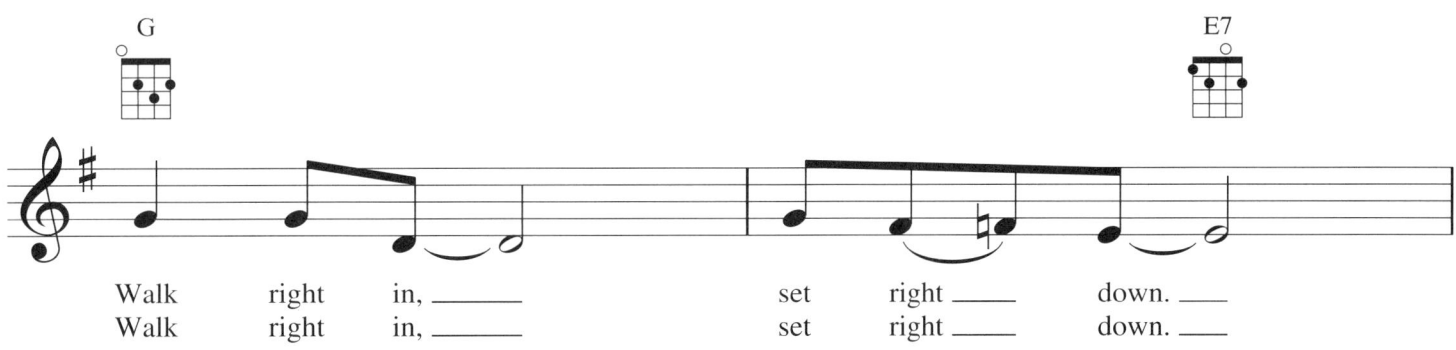
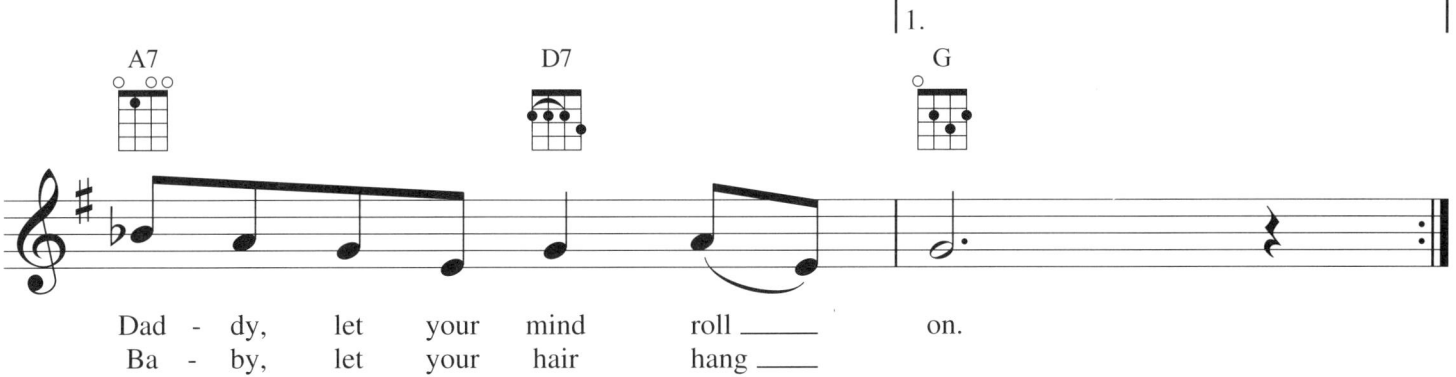
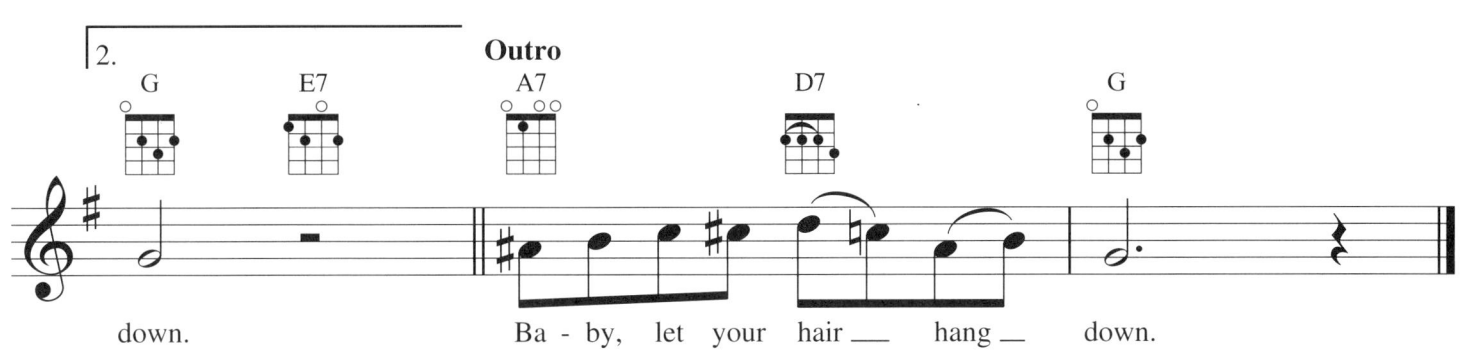

Wishin' and Hopin'

Lyric by Hal David
Music by Burt Bacharach

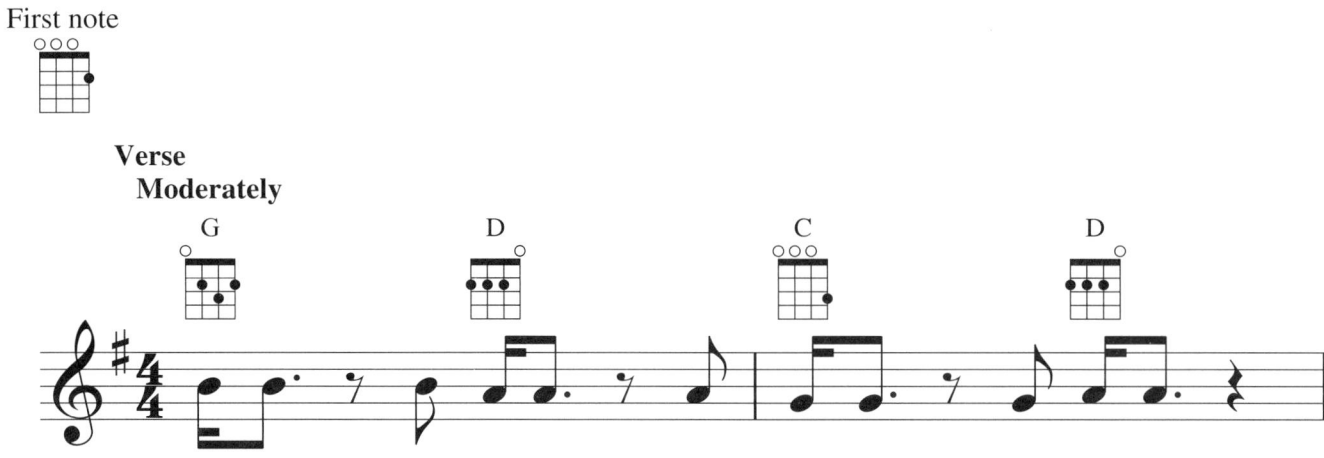

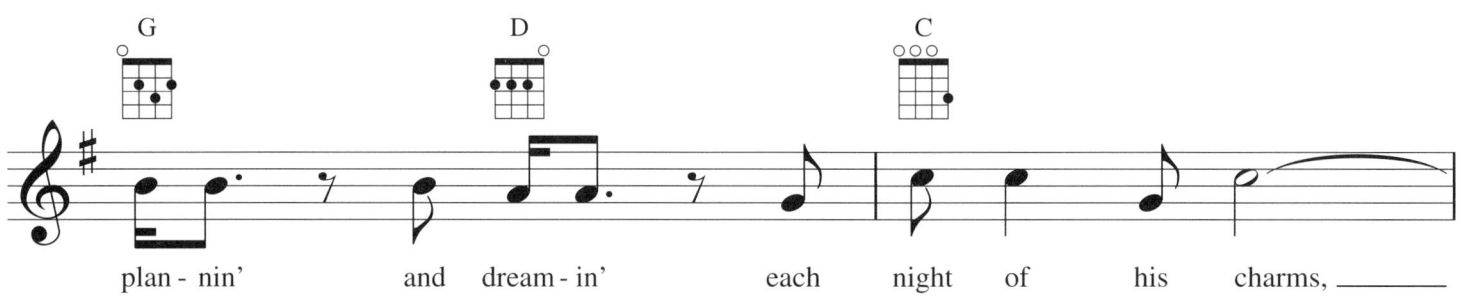

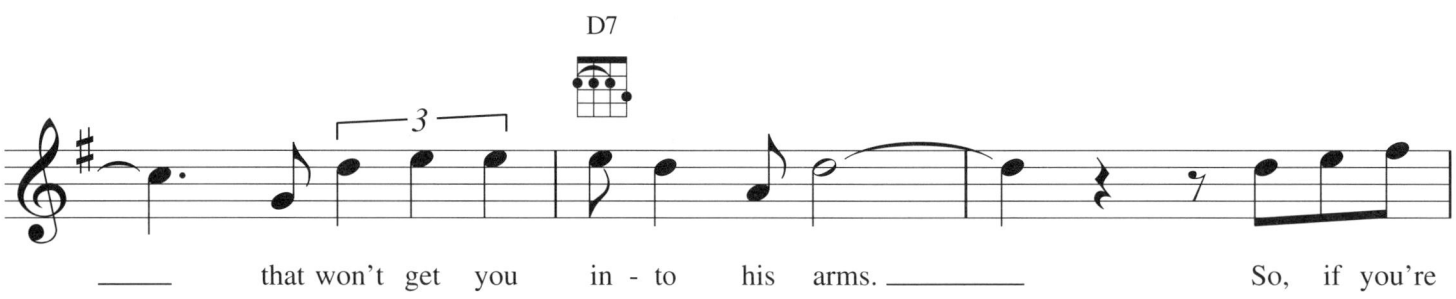

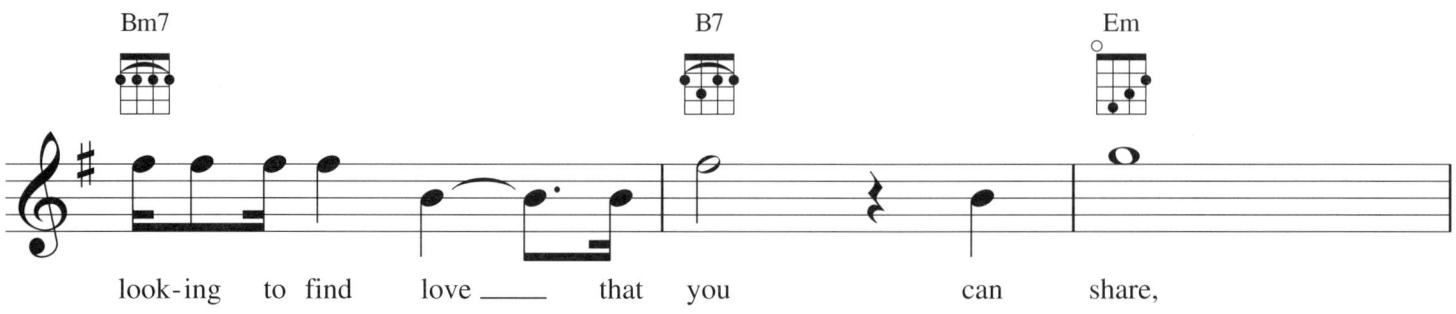

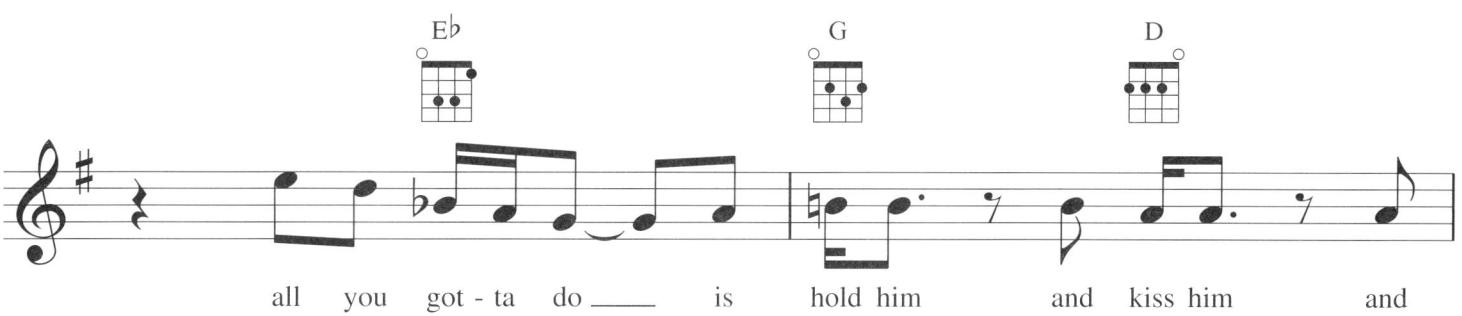

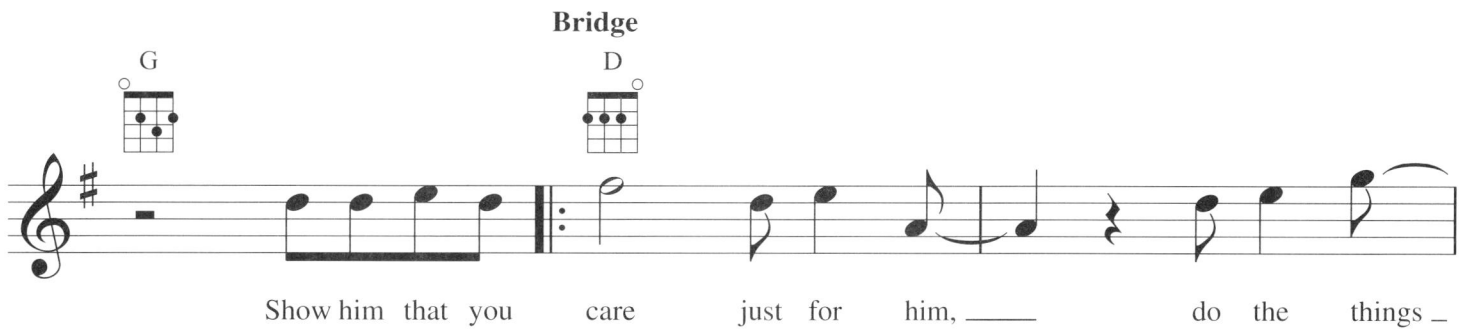

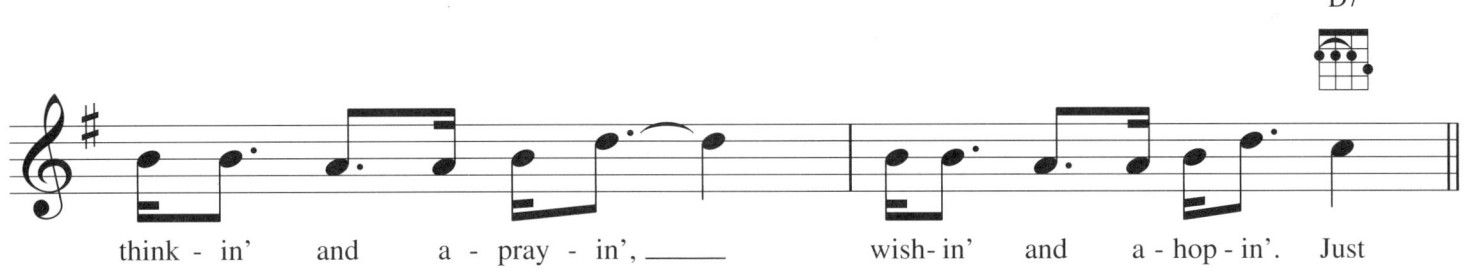
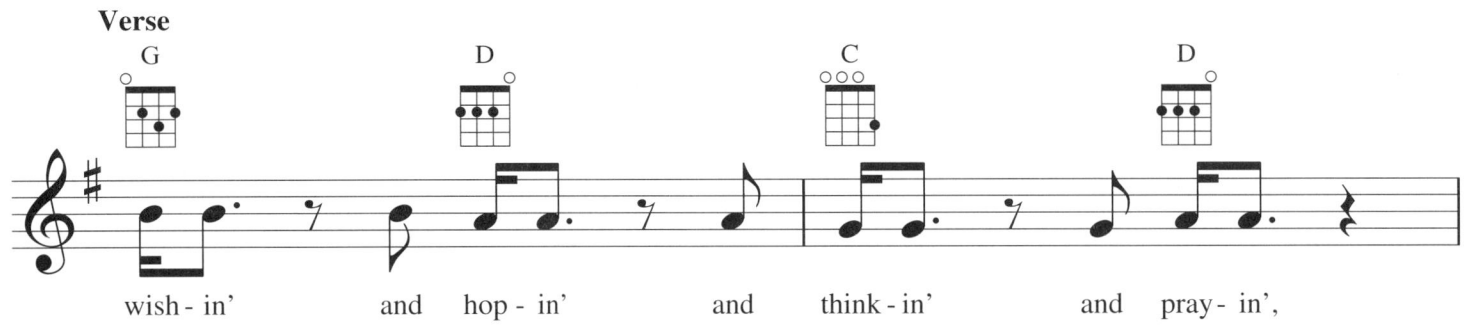

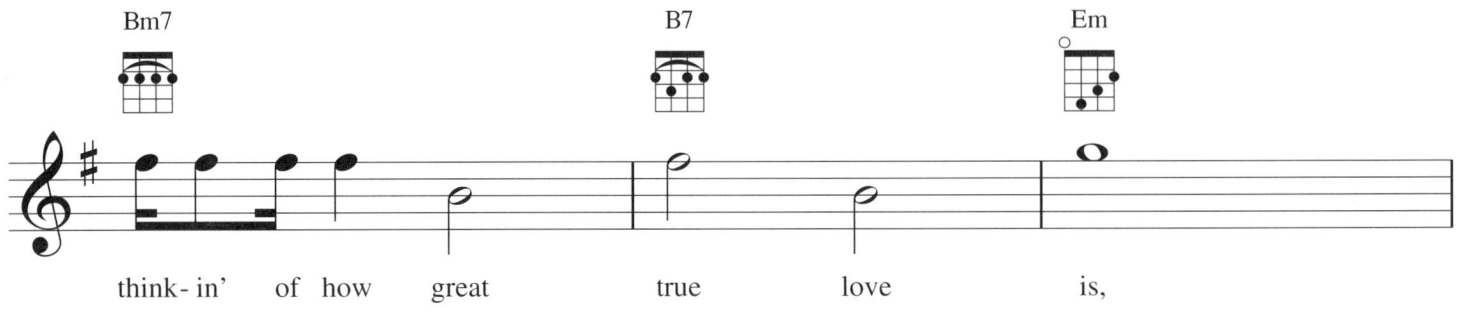

Where Have All the Flowers Gone?

Words and Music by Pete Seeger

First note

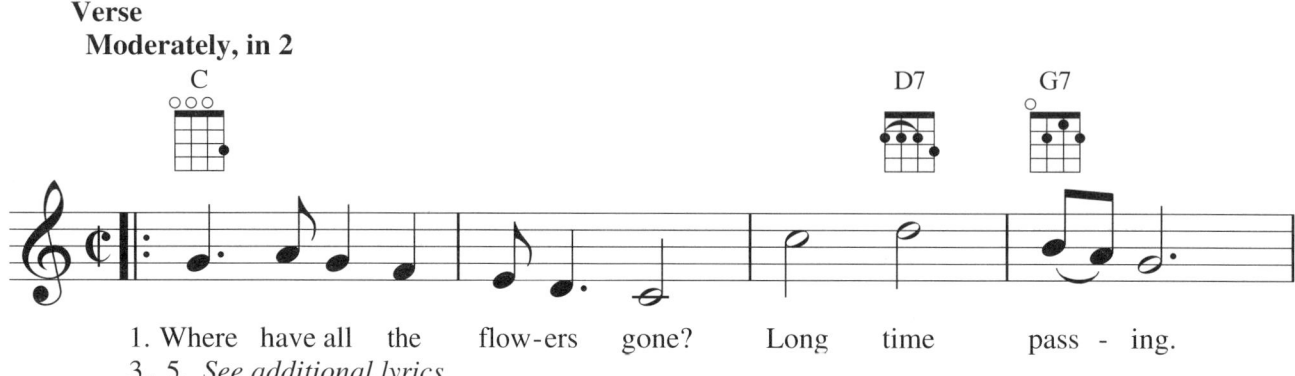

1. Where have all the flow-ers gone? Long time pass-ing.
3., 5. *See additional lyrics*

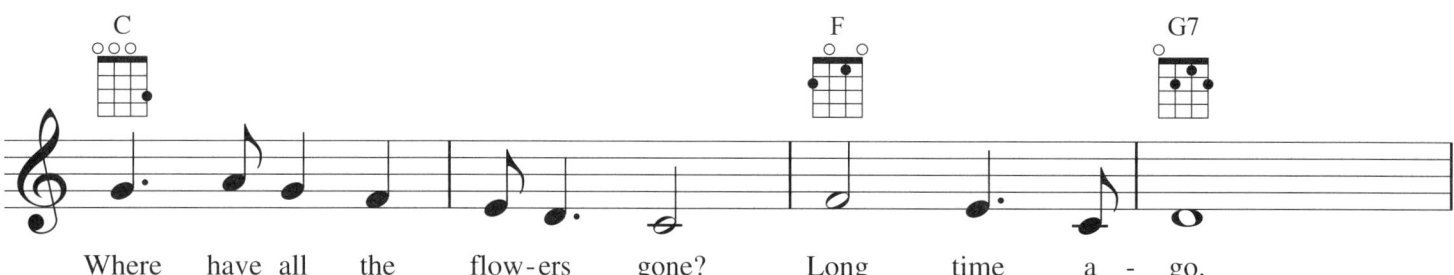

Where have all the flow-ers gone? Long time a-go.

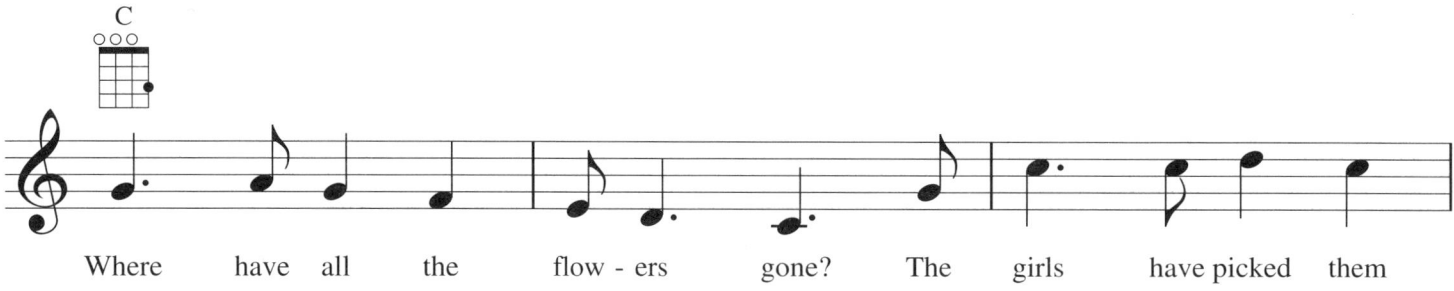

Where have all the flow-ers gone? The girls have picked them

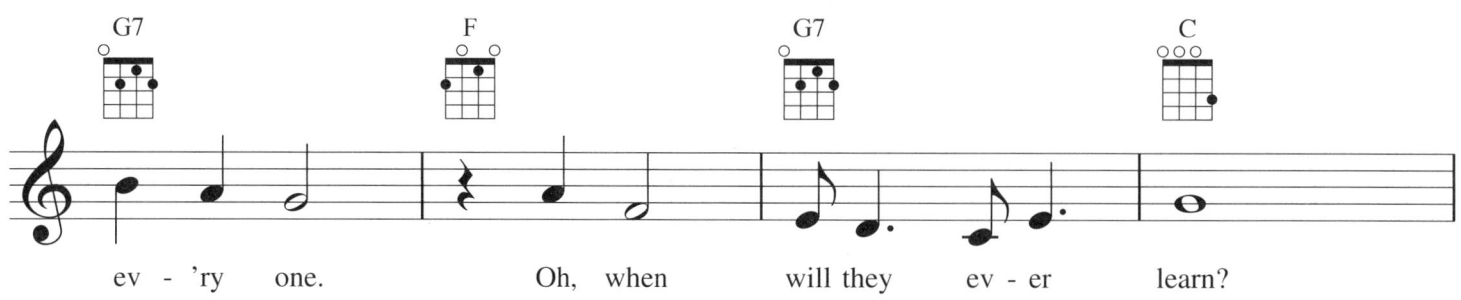

ev-'ry one. Oh, when will they ev-er learn?

Copyright © 1961 (Renewed) by Sanga Music, Inc.
All Rights Reserved   Used by Permission

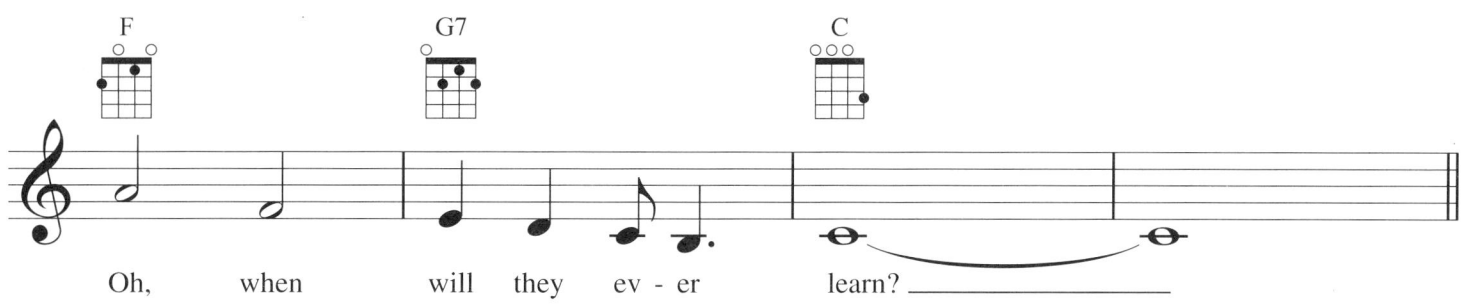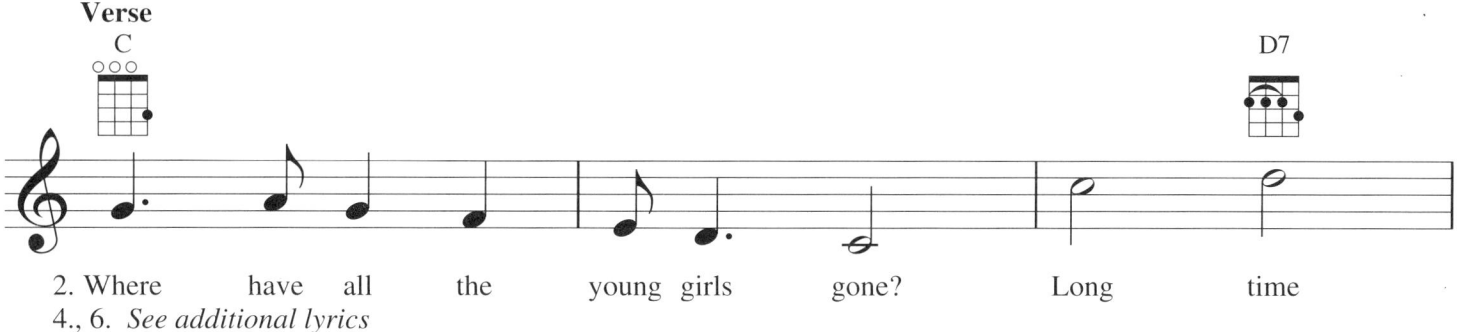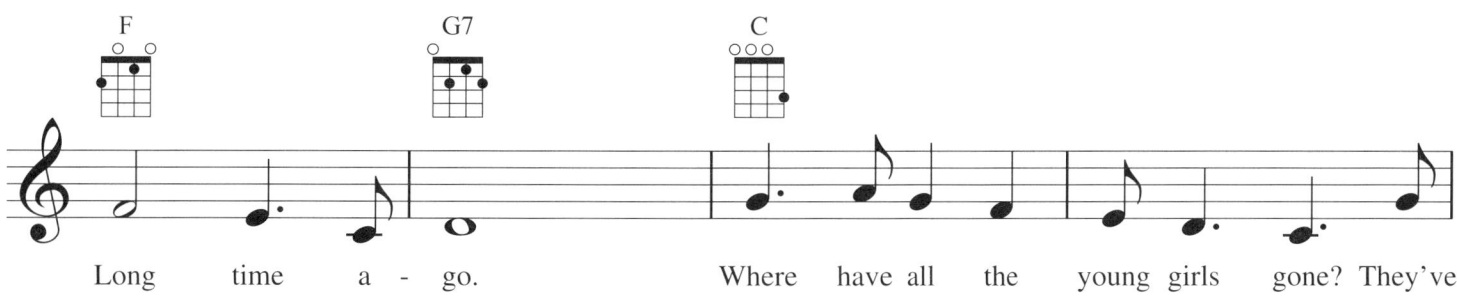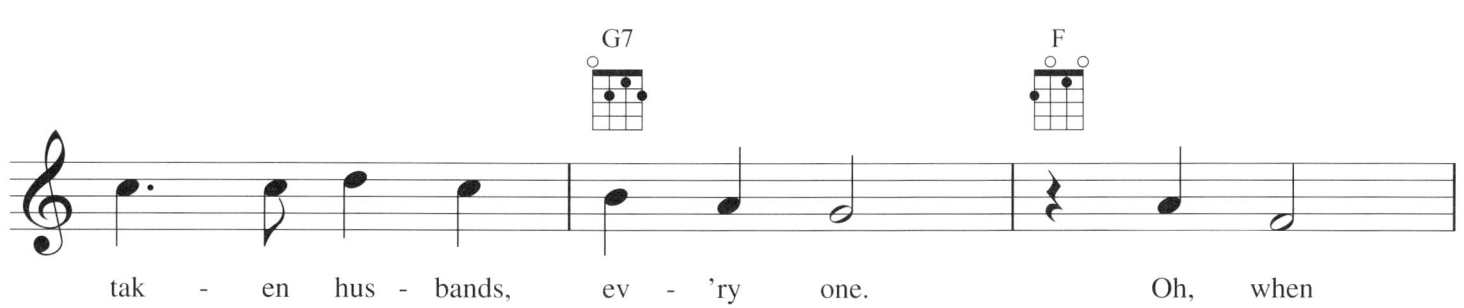

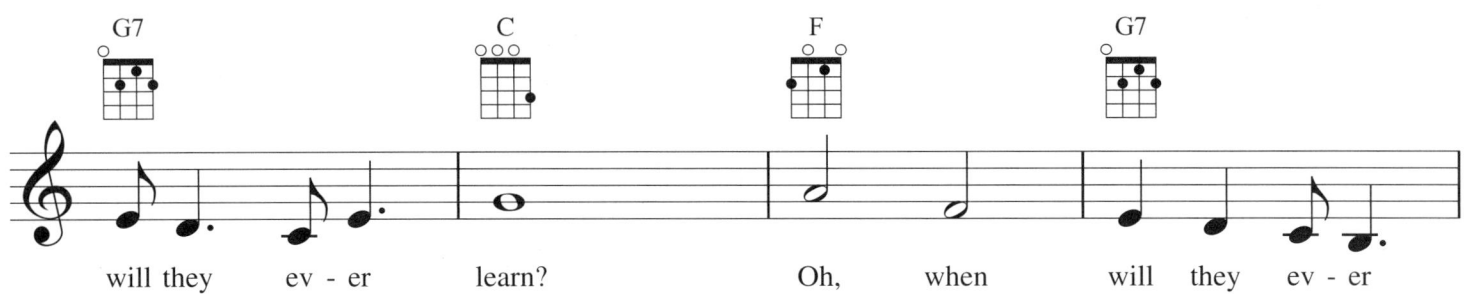
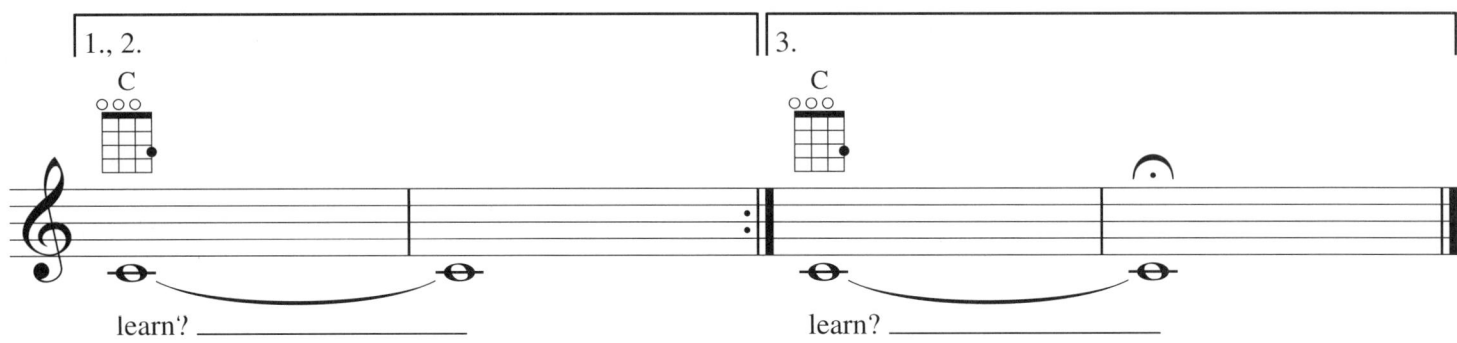

Additional Lyrics

3. Where have all the young men gone? Long time passing.
   Where have all the young men gone? Long time ago.
   Where have all the young men gone?
   They're all in uniform.
   Oh, when will they ever learn?
   Oh, when will they ever learn?

4. Where have all the soldiers gone? Long time passing.
   Where have all the soldiers gone? Long time ago.
   Where have all the soldiers gone?
   They've gone to graveyards, every one.
   Oh, when will they ever learn?
   Oh, when will they ever learn?

5. Where have all the graveyards gone? Long time passing.
   Where have all the graveyards gone? Long time ago.
   Where have all the graveyards gone?
   They're covered with flowers, every one.
   Oh, when will they ever learn?
   Oh, when will they ever learn?

6. Where have all the flowers gone? Long time passing.
   Where have all the flowers gone? Long time ago.
   Where have all the flowers gone?
   Young girls picked them, every one.
   Oh, when will they ever learn?
   Oh, when will they ever learn?

HAL·LEONARD UKULELE PLAY-ALONG

Now you can play your favorite songs on your uke with great-sounding backing tracks to help you sound like a bona fide pro!

1. POP HITS
American Pie • Copacabana (At the Copa) • Crocodile Rock • Kokomo • Lean on Me • Stand by Me • Twist and Shout • What the World Needs Now Is Love.
00701451 Book/CD Pack.........................$14.99

2. UKE CLASSICS
Ain't She Sweet • Five Foot Two, Eyes of Blue (Has Anybody Seen My Girl?) • It's Only a Paper Moon • Living in the Sunlight, Loving in the Moonlight • Pennies from Heaven • Tonight You Belong to Me • Ukulele Lady • When I'm Cleaning Windows.
00701452 Book/CD Pack.........................$12.99

3. HAWAIIAN FAVORITES
Aloha Oe • Blue Hawaii • HarborLights • The Hawaiian Wedding Song (Ke Kali Nei Au) • Mele Kalikimaka • Sleepy Lagoon • Sweet Someone • Tiny Bubbles.
00701453 Book/CD Pack.........................$12.99

4. CHILDREN'S SONGS
Do-Re-Mi • The Hokey Pokey • It's a Small World • My Favorite Things • Puff the Magic Dragon • Sesame Street Theme • Splish Splash • This Land Is Your Land.
00701454 Book/CD Pack.........................$12.99

5. CHRISTMAS SONGS
Do You Hear What I Hear • Feliz Navidad • Frosty the Snow Man • Here Comes Santa Claus (Right down Santa Claus Lane) • Jingle-Bell Rock • Nuttin' for Christmas • Rudolph the Red-Nosed Reindeer • Santa Claus Is Comin' to Town.
00701696 Book/CD Pack.........................$12.99

6. LENNON & McCARTNEY
And I Love Her • Day Tripper • Here, There and Everywhere • Hey Jude • Let It Be • Norwegian Wood (This Bird Has Flown) • Nowhere Man • Yesterday.
00701723 Book/CD Pack.........................$12.99

7. DISNEY FAVORITES
Alice in Wonderland • The Bare Necessities • Candle on the Water • Chim Chim Cher-ee • A Dream Is a Wish Your Heart Makes • Mickey Mouse March • Supercalifragilisticexpialidocious • Under the Sea.
00701724 Book/CD Pack.........................$12.99

8. CHART HITS
All the Right Moves • Bubbly • Hey, Soul Sister • I'm Yours • Toes • Use Somebody • Viva la Vida • You're Beautiful.
00701745 Book/CD Pack.........................$14.99

9. THE SOUND OF MUSIC
Climb Ev'ry Mountain • Do-Re-Mi • Edelweiss • Maria • My Favorite Things • Sixteen Going on Seventeen • Something Good • The Sound of Music.
00701784 Book/CD Pack.........................$12.99

10. MOTOWN
Baby Love • Easy • How Sweet It Is (To Be Loved by You) • I Heard It Through the Grapevine • I Want You Back • My Cherie Amour • My Girl • You Can't Hurry Love.
00701964 Book/CD Pack.........................$12.99

11. CHRISTMAS STRUMMING
Away in a Manger • Deck the Hall • The First Noel • Hark! the Herald Angels Sing • Jingle Bells • Joy to the World • O Come, All Ye Faithful (Adeste Fideles) • We Three Kings of Orient Are.
00702458 Book/CD Pack.........................$12.99

12. BLUEGRASS FAVORITES
Angel Band • Dooley • Fox on the Run • I Am a Man of Constant Sorrow • I'll Fly Away • Keep on the Sunny Side • Sitting on Top of the World • With Body and Soul.
00702584 Book/CD Pack.........................$12.99

13. UKULELE SONGS
Daughter • Dream a Little Dream of Me • Elderly Woman Behind the Counter in a Small Town • Last Kiss • More Than You Know • Sleepless Nights • Tonight You Belong to Me • Yellow Ledbetter.
00702599 Book/CD Pack.........................$12.99

14. JOHNNY CASH
Cry, Cry, Cry • Daddy Sang Bass • Folsom Prison Blues • Hey, Porter • I Walk the Line • Jackson • (Ghost) Riders in the Sky (A Cowboy Legend) • Ring of Fire.
00702615 Book/CD Pack.........................$14.99

15. COUNTRY CLASSICS
Achy Breaky Heart (Don't Tell My Heart) • Chattahoochee • Crazy • King of the Road • Rocky Top • Tennessee Waltz • You Are My Sunshine • Your Cheatin' Heart.
00702834 Book/CD Pack.........................$12.99

16. STANDARDS
Ain't Misbehavin' • All of Me • Beyond the Sea • Georgia on My Mind • Mister Sandman • Moon River • That's Amoré (That's Love) • Unchained Melody.
00702835 Book/CD Pack.........................$12.99

17. POP STANDARDS
Every Breath You Take • Fields of Gold • I Just Called to Say I Love You • Kansas City • Killing Me Softly with His Song • Sunny • Tears in Heaven • What a Wonderful World.
00702836 Book/CD Pack.........................$12.99

23. TAYLOR SWIFT
Crazier • Fearless • Love Story • Mean • Our Song • Teardrops on My Guitar • White Horse • You Belong with Me.
00704106 Book/CD Pack.........................$14.99

24. WINTER WONDERLAND
All I Want for Christmas Is My Two Front Teeth • Blue Christmas • The Christmas Song (Chestnuts Roasting on an Open Fire) • Have Yourself a Merry Little Christmas • Let It Snow! Let It Snow! Let It Snow! • Little Saint Nick • Sleigh Ride • Winter Wonderland.
00101871 Book/CD Pack.........................$12.99

7777 W. BLUEMOUND RD. P.O. BOX 13819 MILWAUKEE, WI 53213

www.halleonard.com

Prices, contents, and availability subject to change without notice.

0912

Ride the Ukulele Wave!

The Beach Boys for Ukulele
This folio features 20 favorites, including: Barbara Ann • Be True to Your School • California Girls • Fun, Fun, Fun • God Only Knows • Good Vibrations • Help Me Rhonda • I Get Around • In My Room • Kokomo • Little Deuce Coupe • Sloop John B • Surfin' U.S.A. • Wouldn't It Be Nice • and more!
00701726 . . . . $14.99

Disney Songs for Ukulele
20 great Disney classics arranged for all uke players, including: Beauty and the Beast • Bibbidi-Bobbidi-Boo (The Magic Song) • Can You Feel the Love Tonight • Chim Chim Cher-ee • Heigh-Ho • It's a Small World • Some Day My Prince Will Come • We're All in This Together • When You Wish upon a Star • and more.
00701708 . . . . $12.99

Elvis Presley for Ukulele
arr. Jim Beloff
20 classic hits from The King: All Shook Up • Blue Hawaii • Blue Suede Shoes • Can't Help Falling in Love • Don't • Heartbreak Hotel • Hound Dog • Jailhouse Rock • Love Me • Love Me Tender • Return to Sender • Suspicious Minds • Teddy Bear • and more.
00701004 . . . . $14.99

The Beatles for Ukulele
Ukulele players can strum, sing and pick along with 20 Beatles classics! Includes: All You Need Is Love • Eight Days a Week • Good Day Sunshine • Here, There and Everywhere • Let It Be • Love Me Do • Penny Lane • Yesterday • and more.
00700154 . . . . $16.99

Folk Songs for Ukulele
A great collection to take along to the campfire! 60 folk songs, including: Amazing Grace • Buffalo Gals • Camptown Races • For He's a Jolly Good Fellow • Good Night Ladies • Home on the Range • I've Been Working on the Railroad • Kumbaya • My Bonnie Lies over the Ocean • On Top of Old Smoky • Scarborough Fair • Swing Low, Sweet Chariot • Take Me Out to the Ball Game • Yankee Doodle • and more.
00696068 . . . . $12.99

Hawaiian Songs for Ukulele
Over thirty songs from the state that made the ukulele famous, including: Beyond the Rainbow • Hanalei Moon • Ka-lu-a • Lovely Hula Girl • Mele Kalikimaka • One More Aloha • Sea Breeze • Tiny Bubbles • Waikiki • and more.
00696065 . . . . $9.99

Irving Berlin Songs Arranged for the "Uke"
20 great songs with full instructions, including: Always • Blue Skies • Easter Parade • How Deep Is the Ocean (How High Is the Sky) • A Pretty Girl Is like a Melody • Say It with Music • What'll I Do? • White Christmas • and more.
00005558 . . . . $6.95

Glee
Music from the Fox Television Show for Ukulele
20 favorites for Gleeks to strum and sing, including: Bad Romance • Beautiful • Defying Gravity • Don't Stop Believin' • No Air • Proud Mary • Rehab • True Colors • and more.
00701722 . . . $14.99

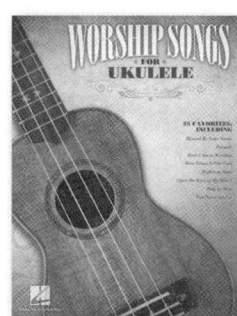

Worship Songs for Ukulele
25 worship songs: Amazing Grace (My Chains are Gone) • Blessed Be Your Name • Enough • God of Wonders • Holy Is the Lord • How Great Is Our God • In Christ Alone • Love the Lord • Mighty to Save • Sing to the King • Step by Step • We Fall Down • and more.
00702546 . . . . $12.99

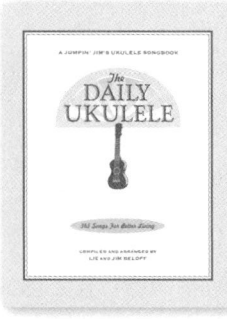

The Daily Ukulele
compiled and arranged by Liz and Jim Beloff
Strum a different song everyday with easy arrangements of 365 of your favorite songs in one big songbook! Includes favorites by the Beatles, Beach Boys, and Bob Dylan, folk songs, pop songs, kids' songs, Christmas carols, and Broadway and Hollywood tunes, all with a spiral binding for ease of use.
00240356 . . . . $34.99

Jake Shimabukuro – Peace Love Ukulele
Deemed "the Hendrix of the ukulele," Hawaii native Jake Shimabukuro is a uke virtuoso. Our songbook features note-for-note transcriptions with ukulele tablature of Jake's masterful playing on all the CD tracks: Bohemian Rhapsody • Boy Meets Girl • Bring Your Adz • Hallelujah • Pianoforte 2010 • Variation on a Dance 2010 • and more, plus two bonus selections!
00702516 . . . . $19.99

Rodgers & Hammerstein for Ukulele
arr. Jim Beloff
Now you can play 20 classic show tunes from this beloved songwriting duo on your uke! Includes: All at Once You Love Her • Do-Re-Mi • Edelweiss • Getting to Know You • Impossible • My Favorite Things • and more.
00701905 . . . . $12.99

Disney characters and artwork © Disney Enterprises, Inc.

Prices, contents, and availability subject to change.

HAL•LEONARD CORPORATION
7777 W. BLUEMOUND RD. P.O. BOX 13819 MILWAUKEE, WI 53213

0212